DISRUPTING
RACISM

Praise for *Disrupting Racism*

Disrupting Racism should be read by everyone. It is a masterpiece. Based on his personal experience, his background as a child prodigy, and his deep knowledge of law and social science, Peter Huang has given an accurate—and wholly empathetic—description of racial discrimination in America (and elsewhere). His characterization of racism leads to sensible and practical prescriptions for how to mitigate this terrible problem—possibly, even to eradicate it.

~ George Akerlof, 2001 Nobel Laureate in Economics

This book throws new light on the damage that is being done by racial discrimination.

~ Edmund Phelps, 2006 Nobel Laureate in Economics and author of *Dynamism* and *Mass Flourishing*

Employing a deeply interdisciplinary approach that combines research from economics, mathematics, mindfulness, and statistics, Dr. Huang's recommendations for disrupting racism are strongly rooted in behavioral science and, perhaps more importantly, they are eminently achievable.

~ Kathryn Stanchi, professor of law at the William S. Boyd School of Law, University of Nevada, Las Vegas

Peter Huang is an incredibly engaging writer. Impeccably researched and delightfully presented, this book is one that every American will want to read. It is a true page-turner that beautifully combines economics, law, psychology, and the study of American racism.

Disrupting Racism helps us understand the connections between economics and race, as well as our connections to ourselves and to one another. It demonstrates the long road ahead as well as the strength of the human spirit, by discussing the tremendous social and economic costs of hatred and discrimination, the effects of positive and negative feedback on recipients, and the importance of love and language.

The book also contains realistic steps that can be taken to help overcome racial hatred. At this fragile moment in society, this book can help us see how fear and discrimination affect humanity and how we can rise above them both.

~ Natalie Martin, professor of law at the University of New Mexico School of Law

Peter Huang is America's modern-day feminist Confucius. His social teachings about the complexities of racism and how to be anti-racist remind us of the mutual obligations we have to each other as one humanity. His appreciation for the psychological costs of racism, combined with the practical applications of economics, mathematics, law, history, and humor breathe urgency and hope into a longstanding social problem that we are each morally required to take part in resolving. Let's heed his teachings and push forward against racism together.

~ Kathy P. Wu, PhD, licensed psychologist

Always the teacher, Dr. Huang educates us on the history of racism against Asians in the US. He explains various theories of racism, revealing that while academically explored, America has significant work to do to eradicate the fear, ignorance, and prejudice that results in racism and discrimination among its citizens.

Dr. Huang explains how racism not only divides Americans based on false beliefs and lack of education, but also how it harms our economy and imperils our health. As all effective academics do, he concludes by describing knowledge and skill-building interventions that could help Americans resist racism.

Disrupting Racism is a key resource in the curriculum all Americans need to better educate themselves about racism, to learn methods for resisting racism, and to work together to create a new normal.

~ Debra S. Austin, JD, PhD, professor at the University of Denver
  Sturm College of Law

From his vast studies of economics, law, and psychology, Peter Huang has found a real-life application for the unfortunately ubiquitous problem of racism. Racism, as it turns out, has many overlooked aspects that are explainable by social science. Add to this unique perspective the telling of Peter's remarkable and peripatetic life, and you have a book that is simultaneously wrenching and delightful to read.

~ Shi-Ling Hsu, D'Alemberte Professor at the Florida State University
  College of Law

Peter Huang offers us a fresh look at racism against Asian-Americans, reminding us of the many-edged mythical "model minority" tropes that the divisive or unthinking in our society force us to navigate. He unpacks the model minority myth, offering insightful and nuanced narratives about the causes and sources of—and prospective remedies for—anti-Asian racism in America.

~ Frederick Tung, professor at Boston University School of Law

This uniquely valuable book begins with a memoir of Professor Huang's extraordinary experiences as an Asian American prodigy. It then sets out the causes and evils of racism and a series of ideas and methods for undercutting it. Throughout, he draws connections between human behavior and experience on the one hand, and, on the other, findings and insights from mathematics, economics, law, psychology—and more. The writing is clear and fresh, studded with examples, leavened with humor, and suffused with wisdom.

~ Leonard L. Riskin, visiting professor at Northwestern University Pritzker School of Law and author of *Managing Conflict Mindfully: Don't Believe Everything You Think*

Funny, smart, and eclectic—these words describe the author's account of racism and its antidote. *Disrupting Racism* is part memoir and part scholarly overview. The intimate portrayal of the polymath mind of the author, a wonder boy who spent his teen years studying with leading thinkers in the Ivy League, takes the reader on a personal tour of the interconnected web of ideas that connects math, behavioral economics, law, and emotion. The journey culminates in an illuminating analysis of institutional and interpersonal racism. This scholarly review of racism is erudite. It weaves together cutting-edge scholarship in Asian American and critical race studies with core concepts in behavioral economics, such as belief-based utility. The book is also practical. It presents ideas for challenging explicit racism by improving racial beliefs and recounting breakthroughs in law and positive psychology that suggest educational strategies to effectively disrupt racism.

~ Ming H. Chen, PhD, JD, professor at University of California Law, San Francisco

This is the story of an extraordinary math prodigy who grew up to be an equally gifted observer of human behavior, as well as a prolific and renowned law professor. What Professor Huang offers in *Disrupting Racism* is one of the clearest and most accessible books on how racism operates, what fuels different types of racism, and how laws can help combat them. Weaving together Shakespeare, behavioral economics, and race as lived experience, Professor Huang examines racism through the lenses of statistical decision theory, cognitive neuroscience, and psychological game theory. It is all immensely readable, and his hilarious conversations with his "tiger mom" are sprinkled throughout the book.

~ Nancy Levit, professor of law at the University of Missouri, Kansas City and coauthor of *The Happy Lawyer*

At this critical time, when our national commitments to civil rights and racial equality are all being called into question, Dr.

Huang provides a much needed perspective. Who better than a former mathematics child prodigy turned legal expert polymath to illuminate that even extraordinary excellence cannot protect an Asian American, let alone other racial groups? All future considerations of diversity, equity, and inclusion policies will need to consult the insights and proposals of *Disrupting Racism* in the important pursuit of eradicating racism.

> ~ Tanya Kateri Hernandez, professor at Fordham University School of Law and author of *Racial Innocence: Unmasking Latino Anti-Black Bias and the Struggle for Equality*

Drawing from an unusually wide range of expertise, Dr. Huang seeks to uncover the roots and nature of racist beliefs. His essays are, in turn, wise, amusing, and hopeful. Not only does he explain our most benighted impulses, but he also identifies practical strategies for overcoming them.

> ~ Susan S. Kuo, associate dean for academic affairs and professor at the University of South Carolina School of Law

Weaving wisdom from mathematics, economics, and law into this grand narrative, Professor Huang tackles the broad challenges of racism—from the contemporary spike in AAPI hate to chronic patterns of indifference, abuse, and rage that America has directed toward disfavored groups. His thoughtful, challenging, and ultimately optimistic essays are a credit not merely to his family and 'Chinese people,' but indeed to all carbon-based life forms.

> ~ James Ming Chen, professor at Michigan State University College of Law

This book presents a thoughtful and engaging story of coming to grips with the seemingly intractable problems of the law's role in addressing racism, as informed by the author's dual training in law and economics. The book is enriched by a distinctive focus on anti-Asian racism. These insights are deepened by the author's reflections on his personal experiences, which illuminate the operation of broader legal dynamics in the everyday lived experience of individuals.

> ~ Jonathan Kahn, professor of law and biology at Northeastern University and author of *Race on the Brain: What Implicit Bias Gets Wrong About the Struggle for Racial Justice*

Amidst a whirlwind of recent political, cultural, and economic events buffeting Asian Americans, Dr. Peter Huang lays out a series of essays connecting it all together and providing direction on how we can disrupt racism. His sage advice draws from current events, psychology, law, economics, and his personal experiences as a fourteen-year-old student at Princeton. He explains how structural factors in our society support racism and how we can break the cycle. The stories and lessons contained within will be familiar to Asian Americans, relatable to all readers, and invaluable to our society as it strives to navigate a diverse future.

> ~ Justin T. Huang, marketing professor at the University of Michigan Ross School of Business

Drawing from his singular life as an Asian American son of a "tiger mom," mathematics prodigy, PhD economist, and law professor, Peter Huang—with wit and weightiness—offers his unique perspective on racism, discrimination, and prejudice. This is a thought-provoking book that provides insight into the bigotry facing America today, and it offers suggestions (some practical and others perhaps wishful) for dealing with it.

> ~ John L. Solow, professor of economics at the University of Central Florida College of Business

A fascinating set of essays from an Asian American academic who has led a fascinating life.

> ~ Dolly Chugh, author of *The Person You Mean to Be* and *A More Just Future,* and professor at the New York University Stern School of Business

This book is a true reflection of the life journey of an extremely talented and passionate scholar.

> ~ Ho-Mou Wu, professor at the China Europe International Business School and professor emeritus at Peking University

A tour de force memoir and essays about racism that will move the needle on our conversations on identity, greed, and equality. Peter Huang blends moving personal insights with rich research expertise spanning psychology, economics, law, and neuroscience. This book is important as well as fascinating.

> ~ Orly Lobel, author of *The Equality Machine* and professor of law at the University of San Diego

Disrupting Racism: Essays by an Asian American Prodigy Professor
Copyright © 2023 by Peter Henry Huang

Published by Endeavor Literary Press
P.O. Box 51455
Colorado Springs, CO 80949
endeavorliterary.com

ISBN Print Version: 978-1-7368734-6-5
ISBN Ebook: 978-1-7368734-7-2

Cover Design: James Clarke (jclarke.net)

DISRUPTING RACISM

PETER H. HUANG, PHD, JD

ENDEAVOR
LITERARY PRESS

Contents

To help disrupt racism, please consider sharing about this book with your family, friends, and social media network with this easy-to-use link: endeavorliterary.com/disrupting-racism.

Preface

I have spent most of my adult life as an educator and all my life as an Asian American racial minority in the US. As an American, I believe that the US is a wonderful country, one that is full of unrealized potential. I hope that someday race will not matter to Americans, or at least not matter as much. But for now, the US is certainly not a post-racism nation. And, as all the statistics show, Asian Americans have been facing increased racism in all its toxic forms.

In early 2020, as the Covid-19 pandemic began to expand across the nation, we heard some political leaders refer to Covid-19 as the "China virus" or "kung flu." Before then, the most recent popular cultural image of Asian Americans had been from the 2018 film *Crazy Rich Asians*. I like the film, but it is possible that it also generated, albeit inadvertently, new stereotypes about Asian Americans.

As I can attest, Asian Americans are not all the same. For example, I have taught game theory to Stanford University undergraduate economics students, but unlike New York University economics professor Rachel Chu, who is the lead female character in *Crazy Rich Asians*, I am not even familiar with the rules of mahjong. In fact, I learned a lot of Asian American history only recently, while writing this book. I am fluent in Mandarin Chinese, but native Chinese speakers often say that I speak Mandarin with a "hillbilly" accent. So, readers will hopefully read this book with an understanding that I am merely one Asian American out of many, and that we are not all the same.

I was born in the USA, just like Bruce Springsteen. I do not think of myself as a foreigner. Although I cannot control how others perceive me, I do not think my yellow skin defines me and I do not think of myself as a "model minority." Rather, I think of myself as an American who is an applied mathematician, citizen, consumer, investor, laborer, lawyer, mathematical economist, patriot, researcher, scientist, student, and teacher. I strongly believe in autonomy, entrepreneurship, and individualism. I also strongly believe in collaboration, mutual interdependence, and teamwork. Like most people, I am the product of my environment, genetics, culture, history, and society.

I was trained in applied mathematics, economics, and law. This means that various parts of the book introduce and apply economic, legal, and mathematical concepts to the problem of racism. I also write about how to apply psychology, neuroscience, and finance—subjects in which I am self-taught—to the problem of racism. Perhaps because I was educated in three distinct areas, I like to find the connections between everything. This will become clear in the book; specifically, I strongly believe that racism is interrelated to other grievous problems in culture, including greed, lackluster education, sexism, and even climate change. At the start of the writing process, I thought about addressing all these issues in the same book, but I soon realized that such a project would be unwieldy for readers.

I will state here that *greed* is the underlying root of all these struggles. In fact, greed is the common root of authoritarianism, discrimination, economic immobility, education inequity, income inequality, incivility, political polarization and partisan extremism, pollution, poverty, rampant political corruption, skyrocketing health insurance, and unregulated, toxic "forever chemicals." Greed leads corporations to place their profits above all else. Greed leads to an attitude my partner describes as, "Hooray for me and frack everybody else" (HFMAFEE), which harms many people, species, and our planet. A HFMAFEE attitude permeates American culture and comports with American rugged individualism. Greed underlies our cherished personal autonomy and notions of freedom. The HFMAFEE attitude has long been a psychologically comforting cultural value, one that was motivated by faith in Adam Smith's "invisible hand" market system and the resulting laissez-faire economic public policies. I don't address all these issues in this book, but please keep in mind that greed is at the root of racism.

Writing this book has been decades in the making—a cathartic, empowering, and therapeutic process. It is a work of love. The essays are based on careful, scholarly research. Some of the chapters are new versions of research

I previously published in peer-reviewed academic journals. I have peppered the book with funny stories and memorable life lessons to make the reading more conversational and friendly. Some of the advice herein has been peer-reviewed by my young nieces! In the interest of protecting and respecting privacy, I do not refer to family members by their actual names.

To help overcome some common stereotypes about Asian Americans, I start this book with my personal story. The rest of the book comprises scholarly essays related to the nature of racism, the impacts of racism, and how racism can be countered through policy, law, and economics. By blending my personal story and my scholarly work in one manuscript, I also hope to demonstrate that legal action and public policy are tools that, for better or worse, ultimately affect the daily lives of real people, including me.

If you hope to find an overarching "moral to the story" after reading this book, remember that people usually come to diverse conclusions about the same narrative. Here's an example. One of my partner's younger sisters had an eighteen-month-old son while she was also pregnant. Upon seeing his mother's enlarged midsection, the little boy became curious about pregnancy, as is often the case. She decided that her son was a bit young to understand the birds and the bees, so instead she read to him a story about a pregnant rabbit. Her precocious son quite reasonably inferred that his mother would soon give birth to a bunny! Thus, I don't want to impose a "moral to the story" on my readers; I would rather give you space to draw your own conclusions, which you will do anyway. That said, you should be more creative and less literal than my partner's nephew! These are, after all, scholarly essays that address one major theme—racism.

My primary hope is that the book will play a role in disrupting racism in America. My objective is to *interrupt* mindlessness about and toward racism. Even small steps forward matter. As author Richelle Goodrich said, "Small steps may appear unimpressive, but don't be deceived. They are the means by which perspectives are subtly altered, mountains are gradually scaled, and lives are drastically changed." A single drop of water can ripple through a lake, a truth depicted on the cover of this book.

PART I

A MINI-MEMOIR

As I write, the United States is facing three crossroads related to race and ethnicity. First, we have witnessed the mainstreaming into American consciousness of the Black Lives Matter (BLM) political and social movement, especially after the murder of George Floyd, Jr. by a Minneapolis police officer. Second, we continue to struggle with a southwestern border immigration crisis. Third, we have seen a dramatic resurgence of hate and bias against Asian Americans.

Racism against Asian Americans is often overlooked and misunderstood. Many non-Asian Americans tend to see us as a monolithic group, when in fact Asian Americans comprise a wide diversity of cultures, languages, and personal traits. Thus, by sharing aspects of my personal history in part 1 of the book, I hope to help my readers understand not only my experiences as an Asian American, but also more about me as a person.

By opening the window on my upbringing and education, I also hope to help readers see that the scholarly essays in the rest of the book are a direct extension of my educational and familial background. Likewise, I hope to show that all efforts to overcome racism—legal, economic, or educational—are ultimately about caring for individual human beings. Academic research is often presented with a detached style, but I hope this book will show that anti-racism initiatives and policies are not merely theoretical; they always respond to and influence personal lives, for better or worse.

Chapter 1

Early Childhood Parental Experimentation

When people learn that I was a freshman at Princeton University at age fourteen, they often ask me what it was like to have such an unusual experience. Fair question. However, my life was a little unusual before I arrived at Princeton.

When I was an infant, my parents became concerned that I had not yet started to walk. To help me out, they purchased a walking windup toy. They thought this toy could inspire me to walk, kind of like a role model. That approach did not go well. While imitating the toy, I promptly tumbled all the way down a staircase.

My parents were also quite concerned that I might one day take up smoking. Even though I was only a toddler, they gave me a cigarette to smoke. That approach *did* work well; the resulting onset of coughing imprinted on me a strong desire to never smoke.

When I was a little older, my mother instructed me to make my bed every morning. I responded by saying that making beds was a futile attempt to resist the second law of thermodynamics, and that the universe was tending toward chaos because of increasing entropy. So, why make my bed?

Before long, I began to see that my parents' best efforts were merely experiments, only without peer-review boards or informed consent forms. They did not really know what they were doing. Some experiments worked and some didn't, but my parents (and I) always learned something, even from the failed attempts.

My grandma also conducted her own experiments. She was born in 1898 and passed away in 2003. When she was sixty, she left Taiwan to come to America to take care of me. She made delicious Chinese dim sum for my after-school snacks: pan-fried *xiao lon bao*, red bean paste buns, pot stickers, scallion pancakes, and spring rolls. When I got home from elementary school, I loved to watch cartoons and do homework during commercials. Grandma used to say repeatedly that no television program could ever be as exciting and interesting as an individual's own life. I took that to heart, and her statement soon proved to be true, at least in my case, but she still liked to watch television.

We had a daily routine. I would set the table before dinner. Grandma cooked our meals from scratch. After we ate, I would clear the table and hand-wash the dishes before placing them into the dishwasher. After that, Grandma and I would watch serialized soap operas broadcast in Mandarin on Manhattan cable television. These shows usually took place in ancient China and detailed how good mythological humans and talking animals, like those in such movies as *Kung Fu Panda*, *Kung Fu Panda 2*, and *Kung Fu Panda 3* could triumph over evil villains and warlords through the power of virtue, creative military stratagems, defensive martial arts, and sheer cunning.

My grandma would also watch American television programs with me, even though she neither spoke nor understood much English. She did this because my mother would let me watch TV if Grandma watched with me, even if Grandma sometimes fell asleep. We routinely watched *Star Trek*, the classic original series. During its first season, when I was eight years old, we saw an episode that featured the Horta, an intelligent silicon-based species that was indigenous to a planet called Janus VI. I was fascinated by the idea of noncarbon life forms, so I asked Mom about whether this was possible. Always willing to encourage my curiosity and learning, she used the opportunity to discuss the definition of biological life and the periodic table.

One weekend my parents took our whole family to a local supermarket. As we passed by the breakfast cereal aisle, I wanted to buy a sugary model because it contained a surprise toy inside the box. The toy in question was not educational, so my mother said no. I did what many eight-year-old kids in that situation would have done: I whined in a desperate and futile attempt to get my way. When that did not work, I initiated a sit-down protest in the middle of the cereal aisle. My mother was not amused. She doubled down on not buying the sugary breakfast cereal with the non-educational surprise toy, and she let me know that, because of my inappropriate behavior in the store aisle, I had embarrassed myself, my mother, my entire immediate family, all Chinese people, all Asian people, all humans, and all carbon-based life forms.

To most Asians, losing face is a terrible experience. Thus, the fear of embarrassment became a great motivator to never engage in behavior that might cause public humiliation. When I misbehaved, my mom frequently told me that I was embarrassing my family, the Chinese race, and all carbon-based life forms.

Mom also made clear to the family that almost all presents given to me had to be educational. For example, my mother approved when my aunt and uncle #4 gave me mathematics flash cards for my sixth birthday. (In Chinese, it is customary to number your aunts and uncles by their birth order, and there are different words for your mother's sister and your mother's brother's wife.) I then happily and proudly took those flash cards to school for classroom show-and-tell in first grade. Not surprisingly, I became the subject of much teasing, and I became the primary target during a dodgeball game that day at recess. However, I learned an important life lesson: It is okay to be interested in and like things that other people may not be excited about, and it is okay if people make fun of you because of those interests.

That lesson stuck with me. As an adult, I tried to convey this invaluable principle to my partner's eight-year-old niece when she told me that she had opted out of her school's science fair because science fairs were only for uncool nerds and weirdos. I asked her if she thought I was a weirdo, to which she replied in the negative. Then, much to her surprise, I told her that I had always participated in science fairs when I was a kid. We talked about the joy of learning about why Alka-Seltzer Plus orange zest cold formula effervescent tablets fizz, why volcanoes erupt with lava, why boats do not sink until they take on water, and why submarines can go under the ocean and surface again. After our brief chat, she reluctantly admitted that science *might* be cool—kind of like magic—and that it was *perhaps* not weird to like it. Some weeks later, I discovered that my partner's niece was awed by how, due to nucleation, a ten-foot-high geyser could occur just by dropping a roll of Mentos into a two-liter plastic bottle of Diet Coke.

My parents' experiments in raising me were often inconsistent with my grandma's approach to raising me. Each week, when I accompanied my grandma to shop for fresh fruits, non-Chinese vegetables, and other groceries, she would buy me candy, potato chips, soda pop, and sugary breakfast cereals. Privately with me, she joked that I would grow up to marry an heir to a family-owned potato chip business because I loved potato chips so much. Knowing that my mother did not approve of unhealthy food, Grandma would hide the junk food that she had bought for me in her bedroom closets and under her bed. But she always got up early to cook for me a traditional Chinese breakfast of handmade dim sum or wonton noodle soup.

So, as a general rule, my mother's experimental

methods involved negative-emotion motivators, whereas my grandmother usually used positive-emotion motivators. My reaction to my mother's technique was to avoid grocery shopping with her. I also learned that, at least in my case, negative-emotion motivators were less effective than positive-emotion motivators.

I did not know it at the time, but these conclusions of mine were supported by behavioral economists George Loewenstein and Ted O'Donoghue who pointed out that there is a potentially high cost to relying on negative emotions to motivate behavior. Specifically, people feel ashamed when attempts at self-control fail, as they invariably do. The experience of shame after failing to achieve a desired behavior is what economists call a "deadweight loss." Law professor Clark Freshman in conjunction with psychologists Adele Hayes and Greg Feldman found that, among law students, *positive* emotions and emotional habits predicted: (1) success at negotiation; (2) success in terms of law school class rank and course grades; and (3) success in terms of emotional health. They also found that negative emotions and emotional habits had the opposite associated correlations.

Even when hearing my mother's admonitions and corrections, I knew that she loved me. As I grew older, we began to spar in a light-hearted manner. I learned that my ability to think quickly was an excellent defense mechanism. For example, my mother would often say that her disciplinary tactics hurt her more than they hurt me. I knew that this statement assumed the validity of an interpersonal comparison of utilities, which is an empirically difficult proposition to sustain. I also told her that if she stopped disciplining me, we would both be better off.

~

I grew up and went to school in New York City, which my mother still thinks is the center of the universe. At age six, in the first grade at Public School (P.S.) 183, I discovered college rankings. That's because my mom bought me a set of Ivy League book covers. The teachers at the school were dedicated to us students, proven by the fact that they continued teaching during a city-wide public-school teachers' strike. Located on the Upper East Side of Manhattan, the school was populated by students who came from upper-middle-class families; my classmates' parents were often physicians, health-care professionals, and research scientists at nearby Rockefeller University and the Sloan Kettering Institute.

Five years later, when I was in sixth grade at P.S. 183, my mom sought to enroll me at Brearley, a nearby private school. The Brearley admissions office employee told my mom that her son could not attend the school. My peeved mom expressed her frustration and told the employee that her son should not be barred from enrolling in the school just because he was Asian. The employee at Brearley told her that the problem had nothing to do with my race;

Brearley, the employee said, was (and still is) an all-girls' K-12 school. My mother's wrong assumption had reflected her experiences with discrimination in the US.

Unable to attend Brearley, I attended seventh grade at Horace Mann School, which is an independent college preparatory school in the Bronx. At that time, it was only for boys. Horace Mann was a lawyer, Massachusetts state legislator, the first secretary of the Massachusetts Board of Education, a member of the US House of Representatives, and a president of Antioch College. In each of these positions, Horace Mann declared that every person, regardless of background, was entitled to a public education based on the practices and principles of a free society. Horace Mann also said that women should have the right to vote, that society should take care of mentally ill people, and that slavery should be abolished. He also had a leading role in creating our American elementary school system.

Later, I developed a crush on my eighth-grade algebra teacher. She was a Wellesley College alumna and recent graduate of Columbia University Teacher's College. She reminded me of the character Jennifer "Jenny" Cavilleri, played by the actress Ali MacGraw, in the romantic and tragic film *Love Story*. I was happy and overjoyed when she paid close attention to my ideas and listened to what I had to say. We had enjoyable, fun, and thought-provoking conversations about logic puzzles, truth tables, and intriguing mathematical ideas, such as the Seven Bridges of Königsberg problem, which is a famous precursor to graph theory and topology. I felt that she was the first person who truly understood me and shared my love of mathematics. I am very grateful to have met her, for she had a pivotal influence in my life as a role model of intellectual curiosity. Inspired by her example, I fell in love with abstract reasoning, analytical thinking, and mathematical logic. On Valentine's Day in ninth grade, I presented her with an equation that depicted a heart-shaped, two-dimensional curve in polar coordinates. She responded to that expression of unsolicited affection with kindness and patience. I also routinely wrote her romantic poems in German (I took German classes in eighth grade), and at the end of homework assignments and quizzes, I often wrote *mit liebe* ("with love").

My mom, however, became worried that my harmless crush on my algebra teacher would distract her number one son from studying. Her distraction tactic changed the course of my life. She took me to see the chair of the New York University mathematics department and convinced him to let me audit the NYU summer school pre-calculus and calculus I classes during the summer between my eighth and ninth grades. I sat front and center in the first row every day during both classes, which were held in the Courant Institute of Mathematical Sciences. I did all the assigned and optional extra credit homework, and I took the in-class, closed-book final examinations in both courses. In their "To whom it may concern" letters of recommendation, the professors wrote that I would have earned an A if I had been officially enrolled in the courses. NYU then allowed me to enroll for credit in calculus II during the six-week second summer school session in July and August of that same year. I earned a course grade of A.

When I started ninth grade at Horace Mann School, there were no mathematics courses left for me to take. So, on my own, I decided to apply calculus to help me understand practically every aspect of life. I even delighted in applying calculus to word problems that involved rates of change. For some reason, I took eleventh grade physics instead of ninth grade biology, and I skipped tenth grade chemistry.

In the fall of my ninth-grade year, at age thirteen, I applied to Harvard, Yale, Princeton, Columbia, and NYU with the hope of starting college the following academic year. I was accepted by Princeton, Columbia, and NYU, but not by Yale and Harvard. Among the schools that had accepted me, NYU was a strong option because I would have been able to finish college in two years and receive a full tuition scholarship. Columbia looked good because I would have been able to live at home. But we chose Princeton because it was the highest-ranked and also well-known for its world-class mathematics department. Off I went to Princeton, feeling ambivalent about skipping the rest of high school.

Chapter 2

An Asian American Child at Princeton

I became a student at Princeton when I was a tween, in part because of a state law related to sex education. New York required all students to complete health and sex education before they could get a high school diploma, but the law also prevented students younger than age sixteen from taking the health and sex education class. And so, due to this catch-22, I became a high school dropout. The Princeton University administrators did not think my lack of sex education would be a problem.

I vividly remember the first day. After my parents dropped me off, I sat alone in a single dormitory room crying and sobbing. My folks had written a letter to the dean of students in the spring or summer of 1973 requesting that I not be assigned like other freshman to live in a multi-person suite because they were afraid that their number one son would be exposed to drugs, rock and roll, and sex. My little single-person room off Nassau Street had a twin bed covered by sheets and pillowcases decorated with Charlie Brown, Lucy, Peppermint Patty, Snoopy, and Woodstock. I had an extra set of bedding with a Winnie the Pooh theme. The room also had a metal bookcase that contained all the required and recommended textbooks for my first-semester courses: Honors Advanced Multivariable Calculus, Intermediate German, Principles of Macroeconomics, and Shakespeare.

During a visit home to see my parents one autumn weekend, my mother inquired about how my classes were going. I dutifully reported on each course. Upon hearing that I was reading *King Lear*, she asked for more details. I told her about the first scene of the play in which King Lear asks his daughters how much each of them loves their parents. My mother apparently believed that this was a compelling question, so she asked me how much I loved *my* parents. I replied by asking her an age-old question, which is depicted in Haddaway's hit song "What Is Love?" She proceeded to define love by describing the following hypothetical scenario.

"Suppose that on a snowy winter day, on First Avenue in Manhattan, a New York City Metropolitan Transportation Authority M15 transit bus suddenly experienced brake failure," she said. "Unable to stop, it runs a red light and careens toward your mother. Suppose also that she had her back turned to the runaway bus. Suppose also that because of severe blizzard conditions and the fact that your mother had both ears covered by earmuffs and a thick scarf, she could not hear any verbal warnings to get out of the way."

Having described that scenario, she asked whether I would love her enough to rush onto First Avenue to push her out of the way of the oncoming bus to save her life . . . even if doing so meant that I would be killed by the bus. Hawaiian singer Bruno Mars answered that question in his 2010 song "Grenade," on the album *Doo-Wops & Hooligans*, when he sang this line: "I'd jump in front of a train for ya." However, I struggled to answer that question truthfully. I knew the answer my mother *wanted* to hear (yes), but I also found the question to be intriguing and paradoxical; it required making a choice between two tragic outcomes.

To stall for more time to think, I asked my mother what she would do if the situation were reversed. She replied by saying that she would not hesitate to give up her life to save her number one son's life. Therefore, because she had just revealed that she preferred to give up her life to save mine, I told her that I would respectfully honor her preferences by not sacrificing my life to save hers.

She was not amused by my logical response. She then countered by asking me if I would answer differently if my future wife or kids had been endangered by the runaway bus instead of her. I answered that I would sacrifice myself to save my kids or wife, to which my mom responded angrily: "So, you admit that you love your wife and kids more than you love your mom!"

For both of us, King Lear's question opened a conversation about love: how to define it precisely and whether it involves the positive interdependence of utility functions. The king's question was infused with tensions about beliefs and identity, which I will discuss later in this book. He wanted the pleasure of knowing that his daughters loved him and identified with him.

As I proceeded through that Shakespeare course, and even further into my postgraduate degrees, I made connections between the king's question and numerous theories in behavioral economics. For example, King Lear's question raises issues about how to account for, analyze, compare, and evaluate judgment and decision-making (JDM), especially in life-and-death situations.

King Lear's question, as I later came to see, also involves what some legal scholars and philosophers call "commensurability." This occurs when people perceive every decision through a cost-benefit analysis. It can be hazardous when people practice commensurability in every decision because some trade-offs (costs) are or should be taboo. For example, suppose that a stranger offered millions of dollars to you in exchange for your child. You would naturally refuse, no matter how much the stranger offered, because you love your child. No amount of money, in this case, would ever be commensurate with the value of your child—if you stick to your principles. Visceral examples of commensurability appear in films such as *Sophie's Choice* and *An Indecent Proposal*.

While I was still at Princeton, King Lear's question also reminded me that actions speak louder than words, that talk is cheap. Actions usually require some type of sacrifice (a personal cost). Later I discovered that this principle is related to the job-market signaling model created by Andrew Michael Spence, the 2001 Nobel Prize winner in Economics. Spence's model explains how accounting, economic, and financial choices might signal private and personal information.[1] For example, economists and game theorists have applied Spence's work to analyze signaling games of asymmetric information, or private knowledge. (If you want to know a little more about game theory, you can watch the movie *A Beautiful Mind*, in which actor Russell Crowe plays game theorist and 1994 Nobel Prize-winning economist John Forbes Nash, Jr.). A growing body of research known as behavioral game theory focuses on how people make decisions compared to how emotionless artificial intelligence makes decisions.

During my conversation about King Lear's question with my mother, I did not yet know that my reasoning also involved what economists call "revealed preference theory." Proposed by Paul A. Samuelson, the 1970 Nobel Prize winner in Economics, this theory deals with what we can infer about someone's preferences by observing their behavior. Behavioral economics and social psychology demonstrate that most people do not have well-formed preferences. Put another way, people will often encounter novel decision-making environments without any clear notion of what they prefer. People often choose what they think will maximize their self-interested well-being, but they often make choices based on the well-being of family members and the search for a sense of purpose. Daniel Kahneman and his frequent coauthor Amos Tversky demonstrated that what people choose often depends on how choices are framed or presented. People will often form preferences to make them conform to perceived life narratives or self-identities.

This one freshman class in Shakespeare opened my eyes to see that our decisions influence not just how others see us, but also how we see ourselves. This in turn motivates us to make choices that can signal to others and ourselves what kind of individuals we are or hope to become. All this intellectual exploration, and much more, took off while I lived alone, often crying, in my Princeton dormitory decorated with Winnie the Pooh and Charlie Brown bed sheets.

~

My first mathematics class at Princeton was a section of honors calculus that mathematics majors usually take in the spring of their sophomore year. The course provided a theoretical introduction to multivariable analysis. A prerequisite for this course was a rigorous linear algebra course that required me to write proofs, like those in middle school geometry. It bridged the gap between single variable calculus and more advanced mathematics courses.

One day, my honors calculus professor announced that our class would not get back our homework assignment because the course's grader had committed suicide. It was rumored that every four years, a Princeton mathematics graduate student, or an undergraduate mathematics major, jumped off the mathematics building, Fine Hall, due to depression, anxiety, or chronic stress. Usually, these emotions were rooted in the pressure to excel academically and/or live up to their own or other peoples' perfectionist expectations.

I had thought little about suicide before that day, but I came to think about it at various times during the next three years, as do many teenagers. According to the United States Center for Disease Control and Prevention, teen suicide is the number two cause of death for youths ages fifteen to twenty-four, which is only surpassed by accidents. Studies show that the constant pressure to "be all that you can be" often exacerbates teen suicides.

It is not just students at elite high schools and universities who have thought about suicide. A fall 2020 web-based survey of college and graduate students found that 13 percent of more than thirty-three thousand students surveyed reported thoughts of suicide, and that almost 40 percent screened positive for depression.[2] A 2021 survey of student well-being distributed to more than twenty-four thousand law students at thirty-nine law schools found that 11 percent of respondents "had thought seriously about suicide in the past year." Nearly 33 percent of the students reported they had thought about attempting suicide in their lifetime, up from 21 percent in 2014.[3]

Many Asian Americans and Asians are raised in a culture where the shame of losing face is to be avoided at all costs, even if it means committing suicide. Constance Wu, who starred in *Crazy Rich Asians* and the television situation comedy show *Fresh Off the Boat*,[4] revealed that she had attempted suicide in 2019 after a social media backlash about her acting career.[5] She felt disgraced after another Asian American actress sent her direct messages that condemned her as a blight on their community.[6] Zeng Ying, a Chinese freelance journalist and influencer based in Japan, attempted suicide after she was cyberbullied for crying during a live report of former Japanese Prime Minister Shinzo Abe's death.[7] She was accused of being unpatriotic.[8]

In other words, there are aspects of the Asian American and Asian cultures that make some people prone to anxiety, stress, and pressures that often lead to suicide. On some occasions during my time at Princeton, that thought also crossed my mind, but thankfully it did not last long. Suicide is always a terrible way to solve a temporary problem. There are always better solutions.

~

After my first year, Princeton allowed me to skip the sophomore year and advance directly to my junior year. I also successfully applied to and became a university scholar, a designation for students with exceptional talents beyond the confines of the standard curriculum. In my third and senior year, I took only graduate courses and reading courses in mathematics, economics, mathematical economics, and politics. I earned my undergraduate degree in mathematics by the age of seventeen.

My junior year independent work advisor at Princeton was Professor Charles Louis Fefferman, a mathematics prodigy who had been a freshman at the University of Maryland at age fourteen. He earned his doctorate in mathematics from Princeton at age twenty, and then became a full professor at the University of Chicago at age twenty-two, the youngest person ever appointed as a full professor in the United States. In 1973, at age twenty-four, he returned to Princeton as a full professor, after which he earned several prestigious science and mathematics awards, including the National Science Foundation's Alan T. Waterman Award and the Fields Medal. The latter is considered to be the highest honor a mathematician can receive—the mathematician's Nobel Prize.

I once had a wide-ranging, one-on-one, ninety-minute conversation with Professor Fefferman on a bus ride between the Port Authority in New York City and Princeton's Nassau Street. We talked about his research, teaching, and mundane things like taking out the garbage. He also talked about his then new role as husband to Julie Anne Albert, a child prodigy in music who studied violin at Juilliard when she was nine.

Fefferman was inspirational, but I realized that I had neither his rare mathematical talent nor his desire to become a pure mathematician. Instead, I had a nascent interest in and attraction to mathematical economics. I had earned, in the spring of that year, an A-plus in Economic Dynamics, taught by a new assistant professor, Martin Hellwig. Taking that course (and earning that grade) gave me the impetus and motivating force to focus on that area.

The course utilized difference equations to model the dynamics of economic systems. Later in life, this knowledge helped to convince me to participate in couples counseling. A related book and article showed me that I could utilize the mathematics of dynamical systems to analyze questions about the psychological factors that impact relationships: emotional inertia, how each member of a couple influences the other, personality, and relationship history.[9]

As my time at Princeton progressed, my interests became more focused. In short, I sought to become a mathematical economic theorist so that I could apply mathematics to economics. This led me to take a course titled Mathematical Programming, which was about linear and nonlinear programming. I also took a pair of graduate mathematical economics courses: Linear and Convex Systems and Advanced Theory. Both courses opened my eyes to a field that possesses the abstraction, beauty, elegance, logic, precision, rigor, and sophistication of pure mathematics but that is applied to analyze important economic and societal issues. It all seemed wondrous. I wanted to apply mathematics to solve economic problems and social challenges. I knew then, or thought I knew, that I would be happy as a mathematical economic theorist for a lifetime. However, life unfolded somewhat differently than I imagined.

Harold W. Kuhn taught both my graduate-level mathematical economics courses and served as my senior thesis advisor. He was well-known for his pioneering research in nonlinear programing, game theory, and algorithms to compute competitive market equilibria. The title of my senior thesis was *Applications of Catastrophe Theory to Economics.* Catastrophe Theory had been invented by French mathematician René Thom to study how dynamical systems can bifurcate. It was popularized by Erik Christopher Zeeman who applied it to biology, economics, and sociology. Zeeman's Catastrophe Theory model of stock market bubbles and crashes was published in 1974 in the inaugural issue of the *Journal of Mathematical Economics.* My senior thesis analyzed that model and other applications of Catastrophe Theory to economics. I have remained interested in applications of this theory to study the stability of general economic equilibria, asset market fluctuations, and aggregate business cycles.

Much later in life, I became fascinated to learn that Catastrophe Theory could be used to mathematically analyze dating, mating, and sudden marriage breakdowns. That gave me peace, because I have always been more comfortable with communicating in the language of mathematics than in the languages of love.[10]

Chapter 3

Three Traumatic Errors in Personal Judgment

As a young teenager studying at Princeton, I was emotionally and socially immature in relation to the more developed and mature students with whom I studied. This occasionally made me prone to mistakes in good judgment. I will share three examples. The first was not related to my race, except that I violated an Asian maxim. The second and third examples perhaps illustrate the "model minority" myth and racial profiling.

On the first occasion, I had recently returned to campus from Thanksgiving break and, as usual, I was walking by myself to the dormitory dining hall. I suddenly heard loud and unfamiliar sounds coming from a closet. Wanting to be helpful, I opened the closet door. What I saw left me embarrassed, shocked, and traumatized. A man, wearing only the top half of a Santa Claus costume was having sex with a topless woman barely clad in a Santa's elf costume!

All three of us were flustered and apologetic.

That image seared into my adolescent memory and left me feeling confused. Like the lyrics from the holiday song titled "I Saw Mommy Kissing Santa Claus," I realized that I had to keep a secret.

In the days and weeks that followed, I felt ashamed that I had opened that closet door. I blamed myself for not following a well-known Asian behavioral norm, which is phonetically pronounced in Mandarin as *bìyào zhǎo máfan* and is translated as: "There is no necessity to go searching for trouble." I also remembered the American idiom about how curiosity killed the cat. Because of my deep sense of shame, I did not discuss this incident with anyone for many years; I shared it for the first time with two therapists while writing this book.

My second error occurred at some point in the fall of my freshman year. Both sections of the advanced honors multivariable calculus course I took had an evening joint-review session in the mathematics department building, Fine Hall. Shortly after attending the combined review session, I started to get phone calls from a caller who asked if I was a virgin, if I had seen a naked girl in person, and if I wanted to meet to have sex. The calls made me feel deeply ashamed, but in poor judgment I did not seek help from an adult. Instead, I chose a self-help approach. I decided to call back and agree to meet her, under the assumption that she would be frightened off and stop calling me. My tactic seemed to work because the calls stopped—just as mysteriously as they had started. I thought I had resolved the problem, which at the time made me feel like I was growing up and developing self-reliance.

However, during the next semester, on a nice spring day as I left my last class, two Princeton University security officers approached me. They escorted me to another location and asked me to write and sign a confession for making obscene phone calls. I was scared. My only memory of what happened next is riding the bus to my parents' home while feeling that I had brought dishonor and shame to myself, my family, and all carbon-based life forms. I thought about running away, but then I realized that would be cowardly and cause my family to lose even more face.

While in a bathroom of my parents' two-bedroom apartment, I sheepishly told my mother what had happened that afternoon, and also about what had happened the previous fall. I was pleasantly surprised by my mother's reaction when she said that she would fight the university's actions against me. That weekend, she also moved me off campus. From then on, I commuted by bus between Princeton and home. On the days when I had classes at 8 a.m., my father rode the subway with me to the Port Authority, where I would begin the ninety-minute bus ride to Princeton.

Prior to writing this chapter, I told my mother that these incidents had deeply affected me, stunting my emotional, social, and sexual development for many years. She had no objections to including them in the book, and she told me that she had always felt bad about sending me to Princeton at such a young age. She was grateful that nothing more serious or tragic happened during my time there. I learned for the first time that she had thought of renting or even buying a place in Princeton so that my grandma could live with and take care of me. My difficult experiences led her to send my two younger brothers to Columbia University— they also started college early—so that they could live at home. And she told me that she had doubts about her three granddaughters going to college at younger-than-usual ages.

After these two incidents, I am happy to say that I never saw women as "heterosexual gaze objects," a phrase I borrow from a Stanford law professor; rather, I always perceived women to be friends. All in all, I turned my attention away from relations with women so that I could focus on academics. I preferred to acquire intellectual strengths rather than pursue bodily interests.

A psychological phenomenon known as the "hot stove effect"[11] provides a sampling-based explanation of how these early asymmetrical experiences in my life shaped my biases, beliefs, and attitudes. Simply stated, a cat that is burned once by a hot stove will learn to avoid hot stoves *and cold stoves*. American author, humorist, lecturer, philosopher, and satirist Mark Twain summarized the hot stove effect in 1897: "We should be careful to get out of an experience only the wisdom that is in it—and stop there; lest we be like the cat that sits down on a hot stove lid. She will never sit down on a hot stove lid again—and that is well; but also, she will never sit down on a cold one anymore."[12] That happened to me; my experiences as an adolescent affected my future relationships.

I learned from these experiences that the hot stove effect also partially explains why racism, sexism, and other types of prejudice can persist. For example, if individuals hold a false belief "that others cannot be trusted, they avoid them, and by avoiding them their false belief cannot be disconfirmed."[13] I discovered that wrong beliefs can be an equilibrium of an adaptive learning process without experimentation. So, it seemed to me that by legally banning discrimination, we could help people with a negative bias against certain groups to interact with those people. In essence, the hot stove effect prevents us from learning about people who are different from us. Discrimination regulations can nudge people to overcome these barriers.

My third error in personal judgment occurred years later when I graduated from the Harvard University Graduate School of Arts and Sciences (GSAS). Just after a lengthy graduation ceremony, I was with my family at the Harvard University Coop, the school's bookstore. While leaving the store with my uncle number two, a man approached me and said he was a Harvard University Coop security officer. Once again, I was escorted to another location where he wanted me to write and sign a confession—this time for shoplifting decals and stickers. He searched me and found no stolen merchandise. Undaunted, he claimed that I must have thrown them away. Memories of that day at Princeton, when I was detained and interrogated by university security, came flooding back, because that earlier horrific and traumatic experience had been viscerally seared into my memory. I am unsure of what exactly happened next, but my worst fear was that I might ruin my family's happiness on graduation day.

I now know what I should have done that day: I should have said nothing, except to ask for a lawyer, and then I should have refused to be involuntarily detained. Like many people, I was only vaguely aware of my legal rights, and therefore I was not confident enough to exercise them.

Over the years, that experience has been a personal reminder that legal rights are not self-enforcing. People must actively choose to exercise their rights, sometimes at great emotional, personal, financial, and reputational costs. In other words, legal rights are what financial economists call "real options." These are analogous to financial options, such as stock options, in the sense that both legal rights and stock options may be exercised or not. Richer people can exercise more legal rights than poorer people. Those who do not fear embarrassment or shame can exercise more legal rights than individuals who fear embarrassment or shame. People with more social support can exercise more legal rights than those with fewer social resources.

For more than a decade, I was deeply unsure about whether to disclose my three errors in personal judgment, a doubt well-expressed by a joke about a man who was so submerged in deep thought that he drowned. They were mistakes, and we humans typically prefer to hide them. However, they presented me with opportunities to learn and grow and improve.

In terms of personal growth, my two encounters with university security likely planted the seeds of a subconscious desire to attend law school and to learn about criminal law—so that I would never again be so petrified and victimized by legal authorities. Now, as a licensed attorney, I am armed with legal confidence, fluency, and literacy. When people try to intimidate me by saying "it's the law," I respond by asking them whether they are referring to federal, state, or local law, and I ask them to share the correct statutory citation.

Hopefully, my willingness to share my painful incidents with the law will inspire readers to learn their legal rights and acquire the confidence to exercise them. And I encourage you to take time to study your legal rights, by doing more than watching movies. In terms of racism and the law, this book will be a good step in that direction.

Unfortunately, the law can't repair the long-lasting emotional and psychological effects of trauma during childhood and adolescence.

The Cost of Adverse Childhood Experiences

All three of my personal judgment errors are examples of the unpredictable and expensive psychic and human costs of trauma during childhood and adolescence. In my case, the traumas in my youth were related to my attendance in college three years earlier than usual. Ironically, my parents wanted me to live in a single dormitory room to prevent me from being exposed to sex. That demonstrates that negative things can happen even when parents do the best they can. They sent me to Princeton early because I was academically capable of excelling in college courses, but I was neither emotionally prepared nor socially ready to interact with adult college students. Those three incidents exemplify the stochastic, incommensurable, and possibly long-term nature of the often-overlooked personal and psychological costs of higher education.

I believe there is much to commend about programs for academically gifted students that enable teens to live together. For example, the Johns Hopkins Center for Talented Youth (CTY) offers in-person, on-campus summer programs and hundreds of online courses for kids in grades one to twelve. (For the record, my mother is not impressed with CTY. One of my cousins attended the school and, according to my mom, "only" got into Barnard College of Columbia University, and not Harvard, Yale, or Princeton.) Another good program for young, gifted students is Mary Baldwin University, a residential women's college with a focus on liberal arts and leadership. Its Program for the Exceptionally Gifted (PEG) allows girls as young as age thirteen to live and study together. One of my favorite people of all time attended PEG. Today, she is a happy entrepreneur, professional, and mother of a six-year-old precocious boy.

These types of programs can be much better situations for young people with advanced academic abilities. They might even prevent the occurrence of what psychologists call Adverse Childhood Experiences (ACEs), which the

Centers for Disease Control and Prevention (CDC) defines as "potentially traumatic events that occur in childhood (age zero to seventeen)." Unfortunately, ACEs happen too often. According to the CDC, "61 percent of adults surveyed across twenty-five states reported they had experienced at least one type of ACE before age eighteen, and nearly one in six reported they had experienced four or more types of ACEs."

Dr. Kathy Wu, a licensed psychologist with a background in treating child survivors of trauma, observed that in our angry, hyperviolent, and polarized American society, there is a national, shared, and macro-level trauma from all-too-common and regularized mass shootings, including in schools, supermarkets, malls, and churches.

Dr. Wu states that in addition to communal and societal trauma, there are many no-less-painful individual, specific, microlevel traumas caused by such factors as Covid-19, hate crimes targeted against minorities, international military fighting, laws restricting the civil rights and freedoms of already marginalized people, and weather disasters caused by global climate catastrophes. ACEs can lead to untreated post-traumatic stress disorder (PTSD). According to the CDC, ACEs "can cause toxic stress (extended or prolonged stress)" and "negatively affect children's brain development, immune systems, and stress-response systems," which can then "affect children's attention, decision-making, and learning."

The monetary costs of ACEs are substantial. The CDC estimates that the "economic and social costs to families, communities, and society totals hundreds of billions of dollars each year. A 10 percent reduction in ACEs in North America could equate to an annual savings of $56 billion." Dr. Wu, in a May 2022 opinion article published in *MedPage Today*, proposed a default approach whereby "clinicians should assume that the child you are treating today has PTSD until otherwise ruled out." She added that doctors and health-care providers should advocate for tighter gun control laws and better prevention against community violence. "All our children are carrying too much unnecessary weight on their small shoulders, and we cannot just stand by and see what will become of them," she wrote.[14]

I concur with Dr. Wu's impassioned opinions about preventing ACEs. The CDC points out on its webpages that fostering "and sustaining safe, stable, nurturing relationships and environments for all children and families can prevent ACEs and help all children reach their full potential. The CDC has produced a resource titled "Preventing Adverse Childhood Experiences (ACEs): Leveraging the Best Available Evidence."

I am continuing to recover from my ACEs, which makes me especially cognizant of, and empathetic toward, the many emotional pressures and mental stressors that today's younger generations face. Many stem from racism and sexism. To ensure the mental health and emotional well-being of children, and to help them become healthy, capable adults, it is imperative that societies develop and sustain trauma-informed approaches to education, legislation, and regulation.

Chapter 4

Texas Tofu, Top Gun Data, and Law School Musicals

A t age seventeen, I enrolled at Harvard University in what is now the John A. Paulson School of Engineering and Applied Sciences to pursue a doctorate in applied mathematics. My principal advisor was Kenneth Joseph Arrow, a recipient of the 1972 Nobel Prize in Economic Sciences. My dissertation is titled *Asymptotic and Structural Stability of Signaling Equilibria*.

Arrow also advised Michael Spence, who was a recipient of the 2001 Nobel Prize in Economic Sciences for his path-breaking research in the economics of asymmetric information, which he called "market signaling." Spence defined job-market signals as alterable, observable characteristics that might affect an individual's unobservable productivity, which can be related to a person's *unobservable* traits. The prototypical example of a job-market signal is higher-education levels.

Spence was agnostic about whether education should be considered a form of human capital. He focused instead on the sorting aspects of higher education signals. Along with Arrow, Nobel Prize-winner Joseph Stiglitz also wrote about how higher education serves as a filter, screen, or label. The traditional view is that higher education increases productivity by helping people acquire cognitive skills and/ or develop soft skills, such as emotional intelligence and punctuality. Arrow agreed with Stiglitz in part, but Arrow stated that higher education does more than signaling. Arrow argued that higher education transmits concrete skills that potential employers value. Presenting data, he suggested that higher education is *both* a form of human capital and job-market signaling.

As I was starting my graduate studies, these debates were swirling among leading economists. I remember asking Arrow why Spence did not study the asymptotic stability and structural stability of market signaling equilibria. Arrow replied that both were difficult and challenging problems in mathematical economics. That conversation helped me choose an interesting, manageable, and suitable dissertation topic. I took Arrow's answer to be a call to action. Hence, my thesis examined the asymptotic stability and structural stability of market signaling equilibria.

Regarding debates about the value of higher education, my own experience with undergraduate and graduate studies proved to equip me with real human capital, not just signaling benefits. In addition to learning from Arrow and

Spence, I also studied under numerous prolific and talented professors. For example, during the spring semester of my first year of graduate school, I had the privilege of taking a course taught by Graciela Chichilnisky, who has two doctorate degrees, one in mathematics from MIT and one in economics from the University of California, Berkeley. At the time, she was starting to apply differential topology methods to analyze social choice problems, which helped me learn about diverse, novel applications of differential topology.[15] Chichilnisky wrote a candid, fascinating chapter about two lessons that she had learned from having to deal with a glass ceiling and gender pay inequity. She reported that women could thrive, succeed, and be happy by turning negative responses into positive resources. She added that the genuine source of happiness is the feeling of being useful to others.[16] Although her research was designed to help women, it influenced my thinking about racial barriers and how to cope with them.

In the summer between my second and third years of graduate school, I went with Arrow to his annual visit to Stanford's Institute for Mathematical Studies in the Social Sciences. On Tuesdays and Thursdays, presenters distributed their unpublished working papers. There were lively debates, discussions, and exchanges about novel aspects of mathematical economics. Presenters ranged from past and future recipients of the Nobel Prize in Economic Sciences, such as Robert Aumann, Paul Milgrom, Roger Myerson, and Robert Wilson. It was exhilarating to have conversations with and learn from them and other intellectual giants in mathematical economics. I also immediately fell in love with the climate, collegiality, camaraderie, community, and culture at this institute.

During the eighth and final year of being a graduate student in applied mathematics at Harvard, my mom asked why it had taken me so long to earn a doctorate. She reminded me that she had earned her doctorate in biophysics in three years while also bringing two children into the world. I responded by saying that I was not physically equipped to give birth to children. She did not find my quip amusing.

There was a good reason for not finishing my doctorate until age twenty-five: During graduate school I was going through adolescence. At age twenty, in my third year of graduate school, I followed Arrow from Harvard to Stanford. I had low tolerance for cold weather, and after enduring three picturesque but frosty New England winters, I welcomed the move from chilly Cambridge, Massachusetts to mild and pleasant Palo Alto, California.

While working at Stanford as a teaching assistant for a section of intermediate microeconomics, my adolescent spirit emerged in the warm California climate. I learned to ride a bicycle, drive a car, play organized six-person volleyball (unfortunately on asphalt courts instead of sand or grass), and date Stanford undergraduate females.

Volleyball led me to accept an offer to be a visiting assistant professor of economics at the University of Iowa during the 1983-1984 school year. My friend John Solow, who had also been an economics graduate student at Stanford, asked me to play on his co-ed and six-man recreational volleyball teams in Iowa. In addition to playing volleyball, I would teach undergraduate courses in two fields of applied microeconomics, namely industrial organization and public finance.

While in Iowa, I attended the annual economics PhD job market meeting, which led to interviews with several university economics departments and government agencies. One interview was with economics professors from a university in Texas. Near the conclusion of that interview, a Japanese American professor of mathematical economics asked if I had any questions about the university. I had been raised to be courteous, so I made a polite inquiry about whether he enjoyed living in Texas. Over the next several minutes, he told me that his wife was happy that she could buy many kinds of tofu in Texas: silken (soft) and regular (Chinese style) and a number of other consistencies. He seemed to genuinely believe that I would be similarly happy to know that I would be able to purchase so many varieties of tofu in Texas. However, his colleagues looked at him in apparent disbelief. He was well-intentioned, but he fell into the trap of assuming that I, as an Asian American, would share his food preferences.

Unfortunately, the Japanese American professor had forgotten a principle of neoclassical economics, which says that people and countries enter trade agreements because they have *different* preferences. Diverse preferences among individuals and nations, according to neoclassical economics, leads to increased international trade. The

51

same can be true on a local or even family level, and even when tofu is involved. To illustrate this fact, Joel Waldfogel, an economics and public policy professor who taught at the University of Minnesota and the Wharton School, once asked his kids and their friends to rank their candy preferences. Then he had them engage in mutually beneficial Halloween candy trading. His kids did not find their dad's request unusual, but their friends expressed displeasure about having to do math before they could eat their Halloween candy.

In another interview, I again saw the trap of assuming that others have the same preferences, tastes, or values. I had been invited to interview for a position at the Center for Naval Analyses (CNA), a defense think tank. The job would give me the opportunity to creatively use applied mathematics to solve real-world problems. I began to imagine working in San Diego while participating in CNA's field program and playing beach volleyball. But during the callback interview at CNA's headquarters in Arlington, Virginia, a CNA research staff member revealed that I would be using real-world data in operations research analysis, including "casualty figures and death tolls from the Falklands conflict." His honest answer convinced me to find another source of employment. I had no interest in dealing with real human death or injury statistics on a regular basis.

During the summer of 1984, I accepted a position as a special consultant economist at the Federal Trade Commission (FTC) in Washington, DC. My assignment that summer was to research and write a paper about multidimensional signals of product quality, such as advertising expenditures and prices. Then, in the fall of that year, my work involved figuring out whether certain city lottery advertisements were deceptive. It was not a glamorous gig.

One afternoon that fall, my mother, after visiting the National Institutes of Health in Bethesda, Maryland, showed up unexpectedly in my office at the FTC. She said that she wanted to watch me at work. I explained that my job was not a sporting event designed for spectators. She agreed to come back at 5 p.m. and took me to a fancy Asian restaurant for dinner. As we finished eating, I asked which hotel she was staying at. She told me that she would be staying with me at my apartment, not at a hotel. I explained that I was renting a one-bedroom apartment in Arlington, Virginia and that she would be more comfortable in a nice Washington, DC hotel. She said that she did not mind sleeping on the living room sofa, at which point I knew that she would not back down from her plan. When we arrived at my apartment, she wanted to check out my bedroom. She saw a framed poster of Madonna playing the role of a club singer in the romantic drama movie *Vision Quest*.

"Do you think Madonna can do calculus?" my mother asked.

"I can do the math for both of us!" I replied.

~

After my FTC staff economist position ended, I embarked on a career in academia. Over the next years, I taught economics at Southern Methodist University, Tulane University, the University of California, Berkeley, the University of California, Los Angeles, the University of Southern California, and Stanford University.

Eventually, I shifted from economics to law. This might seem odd to you, given that I had invested so much time and work in mathematical economics, but there's a good reason. To understand that reason, you should know something about the "research statement," which is required when applying to be granted tenure.

A research statement is a description of what a junior professor plans to do in the near-term future, say three to five years. It is neither a contract nor a promise; instead, it is a summary of past accomplishments, work in progress, and possible research directions. This statement requires the applicant to engage in self-promotion while appearing humble and modest. I did not consider myself to be arrogant or boastful, but I could not help telling the truth about the fact that I was "a wonder kid" who graduated from Princeton at age seventeen—and all the rest. I wrote a humble and modest statement, but I suspect that the professors who evaluated my application might have been concerned. Professors are, like other humans, prone to jealousy.

It is also possible that I failed to adequately communicate my plans for future research, because those who reviewed it said that the statement was too grandiose and unfocused. I know now that I should have stated that I wanted to publish numerous articles about one central problem, but instead I said that my goal was to address three subjects: general equilibrium of incomplete security markets, psychological games of belief-dependent emotions, and law and economics. Thus, I suspect that my research statement was easily faulted for lacking a singular focus.

So, when my application for a tenured position in economics did not pan out, I decided in the fall of 1993, at the age of thirty-five, to apply to attend law school. Why law and not, for example, business? There were three motivating factors. First, my personality, then and now, led me to stubbornly learn about new (to me) fields of study. Second, I saw many of my former economics students succeed in law school. Third, at the time I was watching the Emmy Award-winning series *L.A. Law*, and that made practicing law in Los Angeles appear fun, hip, and sexy.

Off I went to law school. I started at the University of Chicago Law School, but because I felt like an anxious fish out of water there, I transferred to Stanford Law School where I earned my JD. With that degree in hand, I went on to teach law at the University of Pennsylvania, the University of Southern California, the University of Chicago, the University of Virginia, the University of Minnesota, Temple University, Yale University, and the University of Colorado, Boulder (in that order). I also taught conflict resolution at the IE University School of Social and Behavioral Sciences in Madrid, Spain.

Being a law professor has been good to me, for at

least twelve reasons, about which you may be interested. First, the study of law fits well with my upbringing as an American-born Chinese person (ABC). I grew up to have a deep respect for and obedience to authority, precedent, and tradition. Second, watching my maternal grandma practice mindfulness every morning by utilizing mala beads inspired me to be curious about and receptive to mindfulness practices. (You'll see the connection between mindfulness and law later in the book.) Third, I believed that the study of law would help me to address racist violence directed at Asian Americans and to help overcome racism more broadly. Fourth, being raised as an ABC by a "tiger mother" provided me opportunities to respond to her Socratic inquisitions while gaining empathy for people who felt chronic anxiousness caused by perfectionist expectations. Fifth, my ABC upbringing emphasized an Asian version of stoicism, which has led to a lifelong fascination with emotions and emotional intelligence. (I promise to demonstrate to you how that also connects to law.) Sixth, my upbringing gave me the privilege of learning about Chinese philosophical traditions, such as legalism, Confucianism, Taoism, naturalism, and Mohism—they all provided helpful counterpoints to Western legal thought. Seventh, playing the board game of *Go* and learning from Sun Tzu's classic text about military stratagems, *The Art of War*, resulted in a lifelong interest in game theory, which, I promise, relates to law. Eighth, reading the classic *The I Ching or Book of Changes* fostered a curiosity about the predictability of personal, organizational, and societal changes. Ninth, hearing tales about daily food insecurity during military conflicts in China left a lasting impression on me. Tenth, accompanying and helping my maternal grandma on weekly food shopping trips and watching her engage in daily Chinese plant-based cooking, including dim sum, created formative memories that emboldened my desire to foster health and well-being with regulatory policies that democratize access to healthy foods, mindful eating, nutrition knowledge, emotional intelligence, and practical cooking skills. Through the law, I believed, we could foster a healthy, sustainable food culture. Eleventh, my ABC upbringing viscerally demonstrated the importance of cultural and social norms that affect human beliefs and behavior, which often must be regulated by law. Twelfth, and lastly, my ABC upbringing fostered grit, a growth mindset, a love of learning, and enduring belief in the importance of lifelong self-improvement.

All these factors have supported my love of legal research and teaching. It all holds together, and meaningfully so; nevertheless, I can understand why some people think my life is scattershot and disconnected. Even children have wondered about me. My partner's niece, when she was age six, interrogated me about this matter.

"What is your job, anyway?" she asked.

"I teach at a law school," I replied.

"What is law school, anyway?" she asked.

"Some people attend law school after they go to college," I said.

"What is college?" she asked.

"Some people attend college after they go to high school," I answered.

"You mean there is something after *High School Musical*, *High School Musical 2*, and *High School Musical 3*?!" she asked, in shock.

"Yes," I said, "There is law school musical!"

PART II

ESSAYS ON THE LAW AND ECONOMICS OF RACISM

In the summer of 2020, as large public protests over George Floyd's killing erupted, my partner asked me a question: "Why don't you research and then write about whether and how law can solve racism?" She may have been joking, but I took her literally and seriously. I immediately thought about what Martin Luther King Jr. famously said.

Now the other myth that gets around is the idea that legislation cannot really solve the problem and that it has no great role to play in this period of social change because you've got to change the heart and you can't change the heart through legislation. You can't legislate morals. The job must be done through education and religion. Well, there's half-truth involved here. Certainly, if the problem is to be solved then in the final sense, hearts must be changed. Religion and education must play a great role in changing the heart. But we must go on to say that while it may be true that morality cannot be legislated, behavior can be regulated. It may be true that the law cannot change the heart, but it can restrain the heartless. It may be true that the law cannot make a man love me, but it can keep him from lynching me and I think that is important, also. So, there is a need for executive orders. There is a need for judicial decrees. There is a need for civil rights legislation on the local scale within states and on the national scale from the federal government.[17]

My partner pressed me for details on how I might write about laws that address racism. Her persistence led me to think about whether and in what precise sense racism might be like a mathematics problem that can be solved, or that might be impossible to solve.

I decided to first write several law review articles on this important issue as a way to refine my thoughts. While writing them, I made a conceptual breakthrough, most likely due to my mathematical mindset: to think about hate in terms of negatively biased, subjective probability beliefs. I came to see that racism is rooted in a set of subjective beliefs that pertain to how a person might or might not behave. Thus, I increasingly saw the connection between mathematics and efforts to disrupt racism.

The observation that hatred stems from certain racial probability beliefs does not mean that it is easy or simple to change racism. For example, you might know people who believe that Covid-19 is fake, or that Covid-19 vaccines are part of a government conspiracy. Changing those beliefs can be difficult and complicated if people do not desire to change the way they think. This truth is reflected in a joke: How many therapists does it take to change a light bulb? Just one, but only if the light bulb wants to change.

I am not alone in this realization because mathematician and popular author Eugenia Cheng has also written on this connection in her book titled *x + y: A Mathematician's Manifesto for Rethinking Gender*. Based on her mathematical expertise in category theory, she advocates for rethinking the notion of gender. In two video talks, Cheng abstracts from the prime factorization of a composite number to illustrate the concepts of privilege, gender, race, and sexual orientation. Cheng encourages her audience to move away from a set-theory way of thinking and to examine *intrinsic* traits, such as the factors that all men or all women (or nonbinary or gender-fluid people) have in common. Her category-theory approach to relationships helps us to think about, for example, how certain character traits lead us to group humans together. These traits might have cultural associations or statistically observed frequencies in a proper subset of humanity; therefore, they are not exclusive to a *particular* proper subset of humanity.

The essays that follow also integrate concepts, frameworks, and ideas from economics, law, cognitive and social psychology, cognitive and social neuroscience, mindfulness, and statistical decision theory. I believe this holistic approach can better help us reframe, rethink, and resolve a central and thorny problem in human history: racial hate.

In addition to my own research and my personal experiences as an Asian American who is concerned about the recent resurgence of hate against us, the following chapters are also based on Kenneth Arrow's seminal work about information economics,[18] organization economics,[19] mathematical economic models of racial discrimination,[20] and "the scope and limits of ordinary economic analysis for understanding racial discrimination, even in markets."[21]

Other Asian Americans like me have been moved to act, and the next generation is becoming more politically active. They are organizing, supporting Asian American businesses, and voting. Some influential and wealthy Asian American business leaders have pledged and raised $250 million to create a new foundation to challenge discrimination against Asian Americans, collect data to inform policymakers, and redesign school curricula to accurately convey the role of Asian Americans in US history.

It is my earnest desire to help us all resist and

overcome racial hate. Before the Covid-19 pandemic, I had downplayed examples of racism against Asian Americans, but due to tragic recent events, I now see that such a position is naive, unrealistic, and untenable. The Center for the Study of Hate and Extremism reported a 339 percent increase of anti-Asian hate crimes nationally between 2020 and 2021. Explicit racial hate has caused severe damage, harm, injury, pain, suffering, and violence for far too long in human history.

Researchers from Boston College, the University of Michigan, and Microsoft Research analyzed "subtle patterns of consumer discrimination arising from anti-Asian bias." Specifically, they focused on how racism led Asian restaurants in the US to suffer an estimated $7.4 billion in lost revenues during 2020.[22] Other research suggested "that Covid-19-fueled prejudice and discrimination have not been limited to East Asians but are part of a broader phenomenon that has affected Asians generally and Hispanics as well."[23] I hope these essays can help to reduce the human suffering and economic harms caused by racism.

Chapter 5

A Short History of Racism Against Asian Americans

Before the Covid-19 pandemic, I enjoyed dining at all-you-can-eat buffets, especially the vegan Chinese ones. These buffets exemplify the best and worst aspects of modern American neoliberal life: eating at them is relatively inexpensive; you can serve yourself; you can eat huge quantities of food having dubious quality; and you can choose food with an abundant array of colors, cuisines, flavors, shapes, sizes, smells, and textures. Buffets are a one-stop culinary destination for the masses. They give people something that financial economists call "real options," which means that we can enjoy individual autonomy, freedom of choice, fulfillment of desires, gratification of preferences, and satisfaction of impulses. They allow us to pursue, at an economic value, the vices of decadence, excess, gluttony, and waste. To see a visual illustration of these values, I recommend watching a hypnotic four-minute and forty-one-second Sizzler restaurant promotional video from 1991.[24] Also worth viewing is a *Parts Unknown* program during which host Anthony Bourdain eats at a Sizzler with Korean American artist David Choe. Bourdain observed that the Sizzler buffet was "a judgment-free zone where there are no mistakes, a world to explore incongruous combinations, without shame or guilt, free of criticism."[25]

One weekend afternoon before the pandemic, I hurriedly parked my car outside a buffet in southern New Jersey. As I exited my car, the door hit the passenger door of a pickup truck parked in the next spot. Even though my car door had caused no damage, the White female driver of that car angrily yelled, "Why don't you learn how to drive and go back to the country where you were born?"

"That will be a short trip. I'm already here," I replied. Then I thought about, but decided against, asking the other driver to learn to speak more precisely, because learning how to drive and opening car doors are different skills.

During dinner, my partner expressed concern that the angry driver of the other car might use a key to damage my car, or perhaps let the air out of the tires. We decided to finish our meal quickly to ensure there was no vandalism. Fortunately, that did not occur.

This incident, despite being nonviolent, imposed on my partner and me five types of taxes. First, there was a behavioral tax because we had to hurry through our meal. Second, there was a cognitive tax because the incident dominated our thoughts and conversation. Third, there was an emotional tax, the onset of anxiety during our dinner. Fourth, we paid a psychological tax, the experience of anger. Fifth, there was a physical health tax stemming from yet another exposure to racial animus.

When these costs are taken together, we can see how even nonviolent racism can lead to what economists call "deadweight loss," which means that no one benefits from a situation—including the racist. The burden of racially motivated animus will often fall not only on targets of prejudice, but also on those who espouse or practice ethnic/racial hatred.

Racial epithets are unfortunately part of everyday American life. During elementary school and junior high school I was often called a "chink" or "China boy" by some classmates, and by strangers on the streets and subway trains of New York City. My parents taught me to ignore such incidents by repeating the well-known children's rhyme—an irreversible binomial—"sticks and stones . . ." Later, when I was a professor at the University of Iowa, several undergraduates told me they were relieved that I could speak English without a foreign accent.

My father earned his doctorate in metallurgy from the University of California, Berkeley, while my mother earned her doctorate in biophysics from the University of Pittsburgh. But because they grew up speaking Cantonese and Mandarin, respectively, they spoke English with accents. As a result, they faced constant racism. This is also true for immigrants from other nations.[26] In response to these frequent negative encounters, my parents reminded my siblings and me that governments can, and often do, seize real and financial property from people, but that governments cannot take our human capital, such as education and learned skills. They also constantly reminded us that, as Americans, we had a duty to exercise our rights to vote.

My parents also reminded us that we were very fortunate to live in a nation based on the rule of law. They had lived through several horrible wars, including the Sino-Japanese War, the Chinese Civil War, and World War II. They had escaped the Communist rule of mainland China by fleeing to Hong Kong and Taiwan, respectively. These formative personal experiences compelled them to teach us to never take peaceful times for granted and to view racism as a human rights issue.

The dominant American race relations narrative is a Black-and-White binary dichotomy, but American history is unfortunately replete with instances of anger, fear, hatred, scapegoating, and suspicion toward many other non-Anglo peoples, a fact that has been masterfully documented by legal and race scholar Frank H. Wu's book titled *Yellow: Race in America Beyond Black and White*. Asian Americans, like many other ethnic and racial groups, have faced prejudice, stereotyping, discrimination, and racism throughout American history, even though there is a long history of Asian Americans making patriotic, scientific, and technical contributions in the US. Unfortunately, that aspect of US history is rarely taught in public schools or even at many higher education institutions.

"Coolies" and the "Yellow Peril"

Ever since the initial wave of Chinese immigration to America, there has been anti-Chinese prejudice. Chinese men immigrated to the United States in 1849 to work as miners during the California Gold Rush.[27] These workers were called "coolies," a word that Europeans used to describe low-status, low-wage, unskilled laborers in their Asian colonies. Chinese men were also laborers for wealthy robber barons to help build the western portions of the first transcontinental railroads.[28] The Central Pacific Railroad, for example, was incorporated in 1861 by businessmen including Leland Stanford, Charles Crocker, and Mark Hopkins Jr. Crocker recruited Chinese men in California and from the Canton province. By 1868, twelve thousand Chinese men were working on this railroad, making up 90 percent of the total workforce. [29]

After the gold rush, as jobs grew scarce, White working-class men became worried about competition from Chinese immigrants.[30] These fears led to the passage of the Chinese Exclusion Act on May 6, 1882.[31] This was America's first, and thus far only, federal law to prohibit all members of a specific ethnic or national group from immigrating to America. The Chinese Exclusion Act built on the Page Act of 1875, which was named after its sponsor, Representative Horace F. Page, a Republican who introduced it to "end the danger of cheap Chinese labor and immoral Chinese women."[32] Unsurprisingly, anti-Chinese immigration laws incited anti-Chinese violence and vigilantism.[33]

Chinese men were demonized in "images of barbaric hordes of heathen Chinamen wanting to rape White women, which filled the English-language print culture."[34] A *New York Times* editorial on September 3, 1865, said: "With Oriental thoughts will necessarily come Oriental social habits . . . We have four millions of degraded negroes in the South . . . and if, in addition . . . there were to be a flood-tide of Chinese population—a population befouled with all the social vices . . . with heathenish souls and heathenish propensities, whose character, and habits, and modes of thought are firmly fixed by the consolidating influence of ages upon ages—we should be prepared to bid farewell to republicanism and democracy." An earlier *New York Daily Tribune* editorial warned that the US federal government should stop the influx of Chinese, who were "uncivilized, unclean, filthy beyond all conception, without any of the higher domestic or social relations; lustful and sensual in their dispositions."[35]

Such racist depictions, editorials, and images incited vigilantes to burn down Chinatowns and kill the Chinese people living in them.[36] In Los Angeles, on October 23, 1871, an angry mob of over five hundred people brutally massacred and hung twenty Chinese men and boys.[37] They mutilated their corpses in the "deadliest known single lynching incident in US history."[38] From 1882 on, Chinese Americans and other Asian Americans faced "large-scale violence, including massacres in Rock Springs, Wyoming (1885), and Hells Canyon, Oregon (1971)."[39]

Anti-Chinese prejudice later expanded to become

anti-Asian racism. All people who immigrated from Asia were conflated into a single racial category and labeled as "Oriental." This corresponded with the rise of the so-called "Yellow Peril" narrative, which originated with German Emperor Wilhelm II who, after dreaming in 1895 of Buddha riding a dragon and storming Europe, commissioned artist Hermann Knackfuss to depict his dream.[40] The resulting lithograph titled *The Yellow Peril* had the caption, "Peoples of Europe, Defend Your Holiest Possessions," and illustrates an archangel attempting to persuade European nations to unify in defense of women, to protect them from the "attacking" yellow forces of Asia. Versions of this image appeared in the January 22, 1898 issue of the *Harper's Weekly* magazine, with an American readership of hundreds of thousands. Asians and Asian Americans became increasingly seen as perennial foreigners to be treated with fear, scorn, and suspicion.

The "Model Minority" Myth

When World War II and the Cold War started, many Americans feared that excluding Chinese immigrants might damage their nation's relationship with China, which at the time was an ally. This fear led to a shift in Americans' narrative and perspective about Chinese immigration. The Chinese Exclusion Act was repealed on December 17, 1943 by the Magnuson Act.[41] The Citizens Committee to

Repeal Chinese Exclusion "strategically recast the Chinese in its promotional materials as 'law-abiding, peace-loving, courteous people living quietly among us.'" They were no longer seen as the Yellow Peril or coolie hordes.[42] That negative view was replaced by the "model minority myth," another stereotype intertwined with geopolitical tensions, such as the Cold War.[43] This myth was also entangled with efforts to oppose the civil rights movement.[44] The new motivation for lauding Asian Americans was still related to international politics (i.e., to make China an ally against Russia). Once again, Asian Americans were being used for political and/or economic gain. This was neither the first nor last time that would occur.

The false narrative that some minorities are "models" implies that other minorities are inferior to the models. To pigeonhole Asians and Asian Americans as model minorities is to imply that all other minorities are not models. Historically, the classification of Asians and Asian Americans as model minorities was used to pit them against African Americans. This tendency persists today. Those who say there are no more structural inequalities in American society often point to Asians and Asian Americans as being model minorities as a way of downplaying the role of racism in the enduring struggles faced by other racial/ethnic groups, particularly African Americans. The model minority trope therefore divides non-White ethnic groups, all of whom have suffered discrimination, prejudice, and stereotyping.

The model minority myth also places undue pressures

on Asian Americans to excel academically. Jennifer Lee, a sociology professor at Columbia University, and her colleague, Min Zhou, a professor of Asian American studies at the University of California, Los Angeles, have analyzed how immigration laws, institutions, and culture combine to encourage high academic and economic achievement among certain subgroups of Asian Americans.[45]

Susan Fiske, a social psychologist at Princeton University, has found that racism entails at least three social biases: stereotyping (cognition), prejudice (emotion), and discrimination (behavior). She also has found that some Americans feel scorn toward immigrants and envy toward Asians.

Viet Thanh Nguyen, who is a 2016 Pulitzer Prize-winning novelist and a professor at the University of Southern California, points out that the first Asian immigrants were known as "the Asian invasion" and then became known as "the model minority," with the latter being seen as "the desirable classmate, the favored neighbor, the nonthreatening kind of person of color." And he emphasized that "racism is not just the physical assault."[46] Today, despite having the dubious distinction of being a model minority, Asian Americans continue to face violent and nonviolent forms of racism.

In my case, my prodigy status sometimes serves as a "get out of racism jail free" card, but only when my educational achievements lead people to see me as a model minority. This myth shows up in debates over whether Affirmative Action harms Asian Americans or in debates about racial capitalism and identity capitalists.[47] Nancy Leong, a law professor at the University of Denver, coined the phrase "racial capitalism" and defined it as "the process of deriving value from the racial identity of others." She added that it "harms the individuals affected and society as a whole."[48] Professor Leong also coined the phrase "identity capitalists" as "the powerful insiders who eke out social and economic value from people of color, women, LGBTQ people, the poor, and other outgroups."[49]

The Origin of the "Asian American" Identity

The phrase "Asian American" is a label for a politically invented category, one that overlooks the vast diversity within that group. Americans of Asian descent comprise many diverse subcategories of people, some of whom neither share common experiences nor view each other as allies. Yuji Ichioka, an adjunct professor at UCLA and civil rights activist, coined the phrase "Asian American" in May 1968 when he founded the Asian American Political Alliance (AAPA) at the University of California, Berkeley. The AAPA was the first interethnic, pan-Asian American political group, created to unify all multiethnic Americans of Asian descent into a single identity to better advocate for political change and social action.

Since then, *Asian American* has become the standard

expression used by most government agencies, research scholars, mass media, and members of the public to describe people of East Asian and South Asian heritage. This remains controversial and contentious; even the definition of "Asian" remains quite contested. Jeff Yang, a Taiwanese American business consultant and journalist, says this identity is "in beta."[50] Some people prefer to use "Asian American Pacific Islander (AAPI),[51] or the acronym AANHPI to represent Asian American Native Hawaiian/Pacific Islanders.[52]

Although there is remarkable diversity among AAPIs, a single event politically galvanized and unified them.[53] In 1982, a Chinese American draftsman for Chrysler named Vincent Chin was murdered at age twenty-seven by a White supervisor and the supervisor's stepson, a laid-off autoworker. They attacked Chin after a brawl in a strip club where Chin was holding his bachelor's party to celebrate his upcoming wedding. At the time, Detroit's big three car manufacturers were laying off employees due to the success of cars imported from Japan. Chin's attackers mistook him to be of Japanese descent.

Frank H. Wu, president of Queens College in New York, described this explicitly racist incident as an example of double mistaken identity. First, Chin was Chinese, not Japanese. Second, Chin was an American, not a foreigner.[54] The racism, he said, stemmed from the attackers' anger, economic anxiety, and hate. Chin was repeatedly beaten with a baseball bat until they cracked open his head.[55] His last words were, "It's not fair." An emergency medical technician at the scene said Chin's "skull was obviously fractured, there was brains laying on the street . . . Chin was obviously in a fatal condition."[56] A policeman who witnessed his murder said the attacker "was swinging the bat like he was swinging for a home run."[57] Chin was rushed to a hospital, but he arrived in a coma and was pronounced brain-dead. He died four days later on June 23, 1982, after being taken off life support.[58] His wedding guests attended his funeral instead.[59]

The charges against Chin's killers were reduced from second-degree murder to manslaughter under a plea bargain agreement.[60] On March 16, 1983, Wayne County Circuit Court Judge Charles Kaufman fined Chin's murderers $3000, plus $780 in court costs, and sentenced them to serve three years of probation without any jail time. Not surprisingly, the light sentence outraged and shocked Asian Americans. Kin Yee, the Detroit Chinese Welfare Council president, argued that the sentences amounted to a "$3000 license to kill, provided you have a steady job or are a student and the victim is Chinese."[61]

This case became a crucial turning point for Asian American civil rights engagement and a rallying cry for federal hate crime legislation.[62] Tragedy spawned activism.[63] After a while, however, the AAPI diaspora mostly returned to its previous and culturally inclined political inactivity and public silence. It was as if AAPIs decided to keep their heads down, work hard, and mind their own business. In the view of Frank H. Wu, the reaction of AAPIs could be depicted by a Chinese saying: "The loudest duck gets shot first by a hunter." The idea is to "not look for trouble" and "do not get involved." A related Japanese proverb similarly warns that "the nail that sticks out will get pounded." These idioms sharply contrast with the common belief among White Americans that "a squeaky wheel gets the grease."[64]

Pandemic-Fueled Anger and Hate

After the terrible murder of Vincent Chin, anti-AAPI racism existed latently and without political attention. That ended in March 2020 when the global Covid-19 pandemic struck the US. In the film, *Star Wars Episode I: The Phantom Menace*, the sage Jedi, Yoda, famously states, "Fear is the path to the dark side . . . fear leads to anger . . . anger leads to hate . . . hate leads to suffering."[65] Whether Yoda's advice to Anakin Skywalker was psychologically sound is unclear.[66] But it is clear that Covid-19 has fueled fear, anger, and hate toward Asian Americans and Asians.[67]

In his speeches and tweets, former President Trump consciously chose to refer to SARS-CoV-2 as the "China virus," the "kung flu," and the "Wuhan virus."[68] This rhetoric fueled a resurgence of anti-Chinese sentiment and AAPI hate.[69] In addition, he and his backers began to use Asian Americans for political gain.[70] To mobilize his voter base, Trump used the "hate and fear" tactic.[71] Peggy Wallace Kennedy, the daughter of George C. Wallace, the former Alabama governor and career segregationist,[72] recently stated that America's current "president understood, as her father did, that 'the two greatest motivators for disaffected voters' are 'hate and fear.'"[73] As Covid-19 raged, Trump used "kung flu" and similarly inflammatory rhetoric to foment racial and ethnic anger, frustration, and hatred toward Asian Americans and Asian immigrants. Ironically, "17 percent of doctors, 9 percent of physician assistants, and nearly 10 percent of nurses in the United States are of Asian descent. Asians and Asian Americans are also at the forefront of America's efforts to find a vaccine."[74]

These "hate and fear" political tactics have resulted in videos of racist rants on social media against Asian Americans. Other forms of anti-Asian discrimination,[75] harassment,[76] hate crimes,[77] and scapegoating have also erupted.[78] World Health Organization (WHO) officials warned Trump to not use the phrase "Chinese virus"[79] and instead to follow the WHO's best practices for naming infectious diseases.[80] The WHO knew that linking a virus name to a racial group would lead to racial profiling, even when those people could not be blamed.[81] Others also pointed out that the proper way to refer to the disease was Covid-19, which is simple and accurate.[82]

A study analyzing more than 1.2 million hashtags between March 9 and March 23, 2021—the weeks before and after Trump's tweet about the "China virus"—found that approximately 20 percent of the nearly half a million #covid19 hashtags expressed anti-Asian sentiment. In addition, about half of the nearly eight hundred thousand hashtags with #chinesevirus contained anti-Asian expressions.[83] This empirical evidence supports the WHO officials who warned

Trump against using the stigmatizing phrase instead of the neutral, proper term of Covid-19. Other studies support this fact and document the rise of anti-Chinese sentiment on the internet during the outbreak of Covid-19.[84]

The impact of the pandemic on anti-AAPI racism is rooted in deeper aspects of human psychology. Social psychology research shows that humans respond to infectious disease threats with "disgust and prejudice against individuals whose morphological appearance or behavior deviates from normative standards."[85] Stefanie Johnson, a professor of business at the University of Colorado, discusses psychological research that shows how infectious diseases can fuel racism.[86] Even the threat of contracting a disease correlates with ethnocentrism and xenophobia,[87] which can lead to violence against out-group individuals.[88] Americans living in regions with higher infectious disease rates have displayed more implicit and explicit racial biases. The most germ-averse White people exhibit stronger explicit, though not implicit, anti-Black/pro-White racial bias.

As a result, infectious disease threats can fuel anti-immigration attitudes. Humans often behave as if they have a behavioral immune system that causes a strong reaction of disgust against people who look as if they might be contagious or part of a group deemed to have been the source of a disease. Some people even disdain those who are disabled, obese, elderly, or disfigured.

There were 3,800 reported AAPI hate incidents from March 19, 2020 to February 28, 2021, and 68 percent of those were against women.[89] Much of the violence targeted the elderly and vulnerable AAPI subpopulations.[90] Thus, many Asian Americans began to experience a "new normal," the reality that they would not be able to leave their homes unless absolutely necessary and only when protected by pepper spray and other personal-defense devices, such as keychain whistles.[91] Some would not leave home without a volunteer buddy or security from neighborhood watch patrols.[92] Others entered self-defense classes offered by nonprofits such as the Asian American Federation and the Center for Anti-Violence Education.

The rise in AAPI hate and explicit racism included many physical acts of violence by male attackers who yelled anti-Asian epithets and slurs while kicking, punching, and stomping on elderly Asian men and women.[93] There was also the intermediate problem of ambiguous or contested racism, defined as incidents in which some people acknowledge racist motives and some do not. The 2021 Atlanta spa shooting was an example of contested racism.[94]

Attacks on some Asian Americans were captured on videos and then went viral. For example, disturbing surveillance footage recorded a vicious, unprovoked attack in which a man violently kicked an Asian woman in her stomach while shouting expletives and saying, "You don't belong here."[95] The man stomped on her head and upper body three more times[96] as she suffered defenselessly in front of a Manhattan building on the morning of March 29, 2021.[97] The woman had to be hospitalized with "a fractured pelvis and contusion to the head."[98] When the attacker tried to casually walk away, another man chased him, but the attacker pulled out a knife to escape.[99] The victim, age sixty-five, had immigrated from the Philippines to the US decades earlier. The police apprehended the thirty-eight-year-old attacker on Wednesday, March 31, 2021 and charged him with felony assault as a hate crime.[100] In response to this incident and others, many Asians sought to protect their parents from hate.[101] Tiffany Yip, a developmental psychologist at Fordham University, observed that "Black families always have 'the racial talk' [and now] I'm not sure that Asian-American families can avoid 'the talk' any longer."[102]

As a result of these Covid-19 trends, there is now research-based guidance for parents about how to help Asian American teenagers deal with discrimination.[103] There are also resources to help parents have conversations with younger children.[104]

Although I am focusing here on anti-Asian American racism, my analysis also applies to other subgroups who suffer discrimination, prejudice, stereotyping, and oppression based on race, ethnicity, gender, sexual orientation, disability, and weight.[105] This commonality does not deny the unique forms of oppression that diverse groups of people have faced, but there is nevertheless similarity in these hardships.

John Cho, a well-known Korean American actor, observed that Covid-19 has reminded Asian Americans that there is a conditional element to belonging in America. "If the coronavirus has taught us anything, it's that the solution to a widespread problem cannot be patchwork. Never has our interconnectedness and our reliance on each other been plainer. You can't stand up for some and not for others. And like the virus, unchecked aggression has the potential to spread wildly," he wrote.[106]

Chapter 6

Who Gets to Define "Racism"?

White people routinely perceive non-Whites as foreigners. It is not uncommon for White people to snipe at non-Whites by telling them to "go back to the country where you were born." Jennifer Ho, a professor of ethnic studies at the University of Colorado, Boulder, pointed out that non-Whites also endure subtle questions implying they are foreigners. She has grown weary of having to answer questions such as, "Where are you from?"[107] or "What's your nationality?"[108] Ho is "the daughter of a refugee father from communist China and a mother born in Kingston, Jamaica, to immigrant parents from Hong Kong." Most White Americans also have diverse nationalities in their pasts, but no one asks them these types of questions.

From 2020 to 2022, Ho served as president of the Association for Asian American Studies (AAAS), which was founded in 1979 and "has emerged as a primary research and teaching hub for Asian American Studies, an interdisciplinary field born out of the 1960s movements for racial justice and student activism." In March 2020, the AAAS released a statement about anti-Asian harassment and Covid-19 to:

> acknowledge the rise of anti-Asian (especially anti-Chinese) harassment that many Asian Americans (particularly those who look East Asian) are experiencing. As an organization dedicated to the study of Asian Americans, we want to be very clear that xenophobia has no place in our communities or workplaces and that harassment of Asians due to fears of the coronavirus are not only unwarranted but sadly part of a longer history of stereotypes associating Asians, especially Chinese, with disease. We stand firm in rejecting anti-Asian bigotry in the guise of people expressing fear of Novel Coronavirus/Covid-19. We also urge people to find resources that will educate them about how to manage their health as well as why their prejudices/biases in assuming all Asians have the virus are rooted in a history of Yellow Peril rhetoric, xenophobia, ableism, and anti-Asian racism. Please encourage your colleagues and friends to explore this open-source syllabus that addresses anti-Asian bias associated with the coronavirus. And please remember frequent handwashing, not anti-Asian stereotypes/harassment, is your best means of preventing the spread of coronavirus.[109]

Ho developed a wonderful set of online resources "to help educate people about anti-Asian racism that has emerged in the wake of the Covid-19 global pandemic." To do this, she also adopted a scholarly definition of racism, which I have chosen to use in this book. Ho's definition is: "a system where one racial group dominates or has power over others." She adds that racism "is institutional—it is power plus prejudice."[110]

Related to Ho's definition, others have said that "racism equals racial prejudice plus social and institutional power." That last word—power—is important to understand. It refers to institutional and social power, which includes the ability to determine life (economically, socially, physically, etc.) for yourself and others. Power also includes the ability to influence others, to obtain access to decision-makers and resources, and to accomplish desired goals.[111]

If we look closer at the word *prejudice*, we see that it is an "attitude based on limited information, often on stereotypes. Prejudice is usually, but not always, negative. Positive and negative prejudices alike, especially when directed toward oppressed people, are damaging because they both deny the individuality of the person." One example of positive prejudice would be the idea that all Asians are good at math. We could add more nuance to this issue by saying that racism might involve discrimination, hatred, or prejudice; that is, when "one group . . . [has] the power to carry out systematic discrimination through the institutional policies and practices of the society [and by] shaping the cultural beliefs and values that support those racist policies and practices."[112]

There are numerous historical examples of racism in America, including: the dispossession and colonization of Native Americans;[113] the trans-Atlantic slave trading and enslavement of African people;[114] the incarceration of Japanese Americans in World War II;[115] the horrifying detention of Latinx immigrants at southwestern US borders;[116] the ongoing redlining;[117] banning of interracial marriages;[118] and educational racial discrimination.[119]

Racism Uncertainty

Despite having a solid definition of racism, many social interactions might involve subtle forms of racism that make it difficult to prove whether it was motivated by hate. Any encounter with strangers may be "noisy" or confusing, in which case it can be unclear whether there was underlying racial profiling involved. I call this "racism uncertainty."

Those who experience racism uncertainty still incur a social cost. At minimum there is an emotional tax. Social psychologists have demonstrated that people adapt emotionally to events after the fact. They struggle to know how to react or how to explain what transpired.[120] Racism uncertainty can lead to misunderstanding, miscommunication, and misattribution of people's unobservable motives and rationales for their behavior. False assumptions based on racial stereotypes, for example, can lead people to think that an Asian American professor won't be able to speak English without a foreign accent, or even to think that an immigrant is a thief. The following example illustrates racism uncertainty.

During the autumn of 1985, I was a visiting assistant professor at the Southern Methodist University campus near downtown Dallas, Texas. I soon learned that many students drove BMW and Mercedes-Benz convertible cars whereas the SMU faculty would typically drive a Honda or Toyota family sedan. The students' cars fit with the location of the university, which is situated in one of America's most affluent cities. In nearby Snider Plaza, there are many charming cafes, eateries, sandwich shops, fashion boutiques, and other posh stores that cater primarily to wealthy, mostly White SMU students.

After working until after midnight one weekend night, to prepare for teaching a graduate mathematical economics class, I started to walk home from the economics department with some books in hand. A White male SMU police officer stopped his patrol car, shone a flashlight at me, asked me to stop, and requested identification. After complying with his request, he asked what I was doing out so late and if the books belonged to me, implying that he thought I was stealing books. He was not convinced that someone would be working so late on a weekend. After further questioning and seeing a worn copy of a journal article about proper equilibria, he advised me to not work that late and let me go.

Was this encounter a case of a campus officer's

due diligence or was it invidious racial profiling? We will never know the answer. But it demonstrates how racism uncertainty imposes psychological costs: a lack of emotional resolution about potentially racist encounters with strangers. Only that police officer knows if he would have behaved similarly had I been White. I cannot help but wonder what might have happened had the professor been African American or Hispanic American.

Contested Racism

Related to racism uncertainty is *contested racism*. This occurs when some people view a situation as clearly involving racism and some people see that same incident as not involving racism. The question of who gets to say "that was racism" becomes a matter of dispute.[121] Most racists today do not act in seething rage. Their views and attitudes and behaviors are more subtle, at least in public life. This makes racism difficult to clearly define (racism uncertainty) and that leads to contentiousness about racially charged events.

An example of contested racism occurred on March 16, 2021, when "a White man was charged with fatally shooting eight people, including six women of Asian descent, at spas in the Atlanta area."[122] Many news outlets referred to the six victims as "women of Asian descent," even after it was clear that many were Asian Americans. This perpetuated the "foreigner" stereotype.[123] Investigators did not rule out a racial motive for the killings, despite the suspect's claim that he had not been driven by racial bigotry. (He stated that he was trying to eliminate temptations to his sexual addiction.) The contested racism element seeped into legal discussions about whether the man should be charged with a hate crime.

The day after the attack, Captain Jay Baker, the spokesperson for Cherokee County, Georgia Sheriff's Office, stated during a press conference at the Atlanta Police Department headquarters that the suspect "was pretty much fed up and kind of at the end of his rope, and yesterday was a really bad day for him, and this is what he did."[124] After making these insensitive comments, Baker used Facebook to promote anti-Chinese T-shirts. Emblazoned on the shirts were the words: "Covid-19 IMPORTED VIRUS FROM CHY-NA."[125]

Many people, including Chinese American Georgia State Senator Michelle Au, stated that the case demonstrated how "racism and misogyny are intertwined, especially when it comes to perceptions of Asian women."[126] The motivations behind gender bias and racial animus are not mutually exclusive, and indeed are sometimes unfortunately entangled.

The Atlanta area shootings increased the fear of racial violence among many Asian Americans, which had already been increasing since the onset of the pandemic.[127] The killings also sparked outrage[128] and cries for solidarity and unity among minority groups in America.[129] Asian

Americans,[130] who are quite diverse in class, education, and income,[131] collectively pushed for better tracking of hate crimes, greater political involvement, increased multilingual support for mental health, improved legal and employment services, more political representation, and more public education about Asian Americans' contributions to US history.[132]

On March 18, 2021, the US House of Representatives Judiciary Committee held a live-streamed, three-hour hearing titled "Discrimination and Violence Against Asian Americans."[133] It was the first congressional hearing about anti-Asian discrimination and violence in over thirty years.[134] Chip Roy, a US Representative from Texas, chose the hearing to make "a lengthy condemnation of the Chinese government's handling of the coronavirus and asserted that objections to what he categorized as nothing more than hawkish rhetoric about China amounted to 'policing' of free speech."[135] Thomas Miller McClintock II, a US Representative from California, decided to cite two statistics to, as he put it, "add perspective to this issue."[136] His statistics showed that Asian Americans comprise 4.4 percent of hate crime victims, a lower rate than victims who are Black, White, and Hispanic.[137] In addition, he said that Asian Americans have the highest median income among of any ethnic group of Americans.[138] Then he asked, "If America were such a hate-filled, discriminatory, racist society filled with animus against Asian Americans, how do you explain the remarkable success of Asian Americans?"[139]

An obvious response to those statements is that Asian

Americans have succeeded despite living in a hate-filled, discriminatory, racist society filled with animus against us. The success of Asian Americans would be far greater if we did not have to face racial obstacles. Another possible response is that Asian Americans over the generations have often succeeded because we have had to develop grit and resilience to make it in the US.

President Joe Biden and Vice President Kamala Harris have condemned violence against Asian Americans.[140] Biden signed an executive order directing the US federal government "to work toward stopping anti-Asian bias, xenophobia, and harassment." He pressed Congress to pass the Covid-19 Hate Crimes Act, which Biden believed would "expedite the federal government's response to the rise of hate crimes exacerbated during the pandemic." The legislation, sponsored by Asian American US Senator from Hawaii Mazie K. Hirono and US Representative from New York Grace Meng, directs federal officials to review current federal, state, and local hate crime laws. It also establishes online threat-reporting systems to facilitate the reporting of pandemic-related hate crimes.[141] The related No Hate Act,[142] proposed by US Senator Richard Blumenthal, offers grants to states to improve hate crime reporting and permits courts to mandate those convicted under the Matthew Shepard and James Byrd, Jr. Hate Crimes Prevention Act to engage in community service and participate in educational programs as conditions for supervised release.[143]

These legislative efforts are laudable and important, but we need to remember that the underlying causes of race-based hatred and violence are fear, ignorance, and lack of empathy. For this reason, we need to educate Americans about how everyone, regardless of race and ethnicity, has contributed to America's history and economic prosperity. Unfortunately, in the case of many non-White groups, some of their contributions have been forced by oppression: the confiscation of property, cheap or free involuntary labor, and military service. Whatever the case, Americans have to appreciate and understand how minority groups have played important roles in our nation's democracy and political experiment.

An award-winning documentary film about Asian American history, titled *Far East Deep South*, depicts some of the often-unseen contributions of Asian Americans to the US culture and economy. It focuses on how Asian Americans helped freed slaves. The movie reveals an emotional, poignant journey—from California to Mississippi—of a Chinese American man who desired to visit his father's grave. His voyage reveals "the racially complex history of the early Chinese in the segregated South."[144] The film discusses how Chinese American grocery stores sold goods to freed Blacks at lower prices than the inflated prices that plantation commissaries charged so as to keep former slaves in debt.[145] The film reveals that Chinese American grocery shops offered short-term loans to their African American customers, all of whom had no access to formal credit markets.[146]

Statistical Discrimination and the Normalization of Stereotypes

Despite efforts to counter racism uncertainty and contested racism, Asian Americans and other non-White people often struggle with the normalization of racism in America. I know this from personal experience. Verbal racial slights have been commonplace and normalized in my life. I have become less and less surprised by ethnic and racial stereotyping. I have become rather numb to situations in which people make inaccurate prejudgments about me based solely on my appearance or surname. I have viewed such encounters as what economists call "statistical discrimination."[147] Perhaps this is due in part to the fact that I have studied theories about statistical discrimination, including several pioneered by my PhD advisor and Nobel Prize-winner Kenneth Arrow. According to Arrow, "Economic statistical discrimination theory is able to explain how racial profiling and gender discrimination can exist and persist if people use observable characteristics . . . such as . . . gender or race, as a proxy for otherwise unobservable outcome relevant characteristics. So, in the absence of direct information about an individual's productivity, qualifications . . . a decision-maker may substitute group averages (either real or imagined) or stereotypes to fill the information void." He also made clear that statistical discrimination is further exacerbated by people's risk aversion.[148]

Statistical discrimination was intended to be a model

of information-based discrimination rather than animus-based discrimination, but not all economists have agreed. One contrarian is William Spriggs, who is one of the most respected Black economists in America.[149] Spriggs is the chief economist of the AFL-CIO, which is the largest federation of unions in the US, and a board member of the National Bureau of Economic Research (NBER). Fifteen days after a Minneapolis police officer killed George Floyd on May 25, 2020, Spriggs published an open letter to his fellow economists.

Another strain of economists is the 'polite' economists who use 'statistical discrimination' as a way to resolve what they perceive as an agency problem in how racism can affect economic outcomes. To Black economists, 'statistical discrimination' is a constant micro-aggression. It is a model that makes no sense. How does a model assume that an entire set of actors, observing the infinite diversity of human beings, all settle on 'race' as a meaningful marker independent of history, laws, and social norms? And, miraculously, those same 'rational' actors use 'statistical' methods to find only negative attributes highly correlated with 'race.' The fact that far too many economists blindly agree that negative attributes correlate to being African American and cannot see that relationship to police officers assuming all Black men are criminals is stupefying. The fact that a discipline that prides itself on being objective and looking for data to test hypotheses fails to see how negative attributes do not correlate with being African American is a constant irritant for Black economists.[150]

Statistical discrimination is a form of prejudice because it relies on stereotypes, but it doesn't always seem invidious.[151] Some discrimination even sounds flattering. Nevertheless, prejudice appears when people tell me that, for example, being an Asian American explains my educational achievements. These people believe that my academic achievements result from genetics, when in fact my achievements are the result of long-term hard work, grit, and persistence. In addition, people often perceive me as a model minority because I was raised to be humble, modest, and self-deprecating—to a fault. My parents raised me to avoid trouble, to be quiet, and to blend into the background. They made it clear that I should not brag or bring attention to myself. As a result, Asian Americans like me often avoid conflicts, which feeds the model minority myth.

Racism does not always involve an overt or threatening experience. Njeri Mathis Rutledge, a professor of law at South Texas College of Law in Houston and an associate municipal court judge and magistrate,[152] recently realized that her success as a Black woman in America comes from her ability to dismiss or "normalize" the racism she faces daily. She had this epiphany when a White colleague asked her if she had ever personally experienced racism. She reflexively said no because she had never been a victim of police abuse or some other life-threatening racial incident.

Then she realized that she had excluded from her response all the racist slights that had been directed at her. She had in fact experienced racism "Every. Single. Day." She revealed that she was "soul-achingly" tired. "Tired of denying, minimizing, and dealing with racism. Tired of waking my daughter up from nightmares where she's asking me if the police are going to kill us . . . [tired] of a lifetime of conversations about racism, service on diversity committees, and participation in anti-racism workshops . . . [tired] of being terrified every time my gentle, educated Black husband leaves our house, [that] he will be the victim of police violence."[153]

The normalization of racial insults, stereotypes, and slurs "props up a powerful facade of acceptability, even to its victims. Minimizing the daily abusive reality of people of color is in many ways more corrosive to the ideals of equality, and harder to eliminate, than the violent extremes," Rutledge said. "I can no longer normalize the unacceptable. None of us should. If Americans want to build a society truly reflecting our nation's 'self-evident' truths in our Declaration of Independence, we must all identify racism for what it is, working together to ensure a new normal."[154]

Chapter 7

The Fallacy of "Respectability Politics"

Respectability politics occurs "when minority and/or marginalized groups are told (or teach themselves) that in order to receive better treatment from the group in power, they must behave better."[155] Evelyn Brooks Higginbotham, a professor of history and African American studies at Harvard, introduced the phrase "politics of respectability" in her book *Righteous Discontent: The Women's Movement in the Black Baptist Church, 1880-1920.* Respectability politics is based on the belief that being respectable will somehow magically solve the problems of bigotry, oppression, and racism. Sadly, this assumption is demonstrably and empirically false.[156] Behaving respectably does not guarantee minorities any safety from even low-level, nonviolent racism, let alone violent forms of racism. Any "safety" is at best contingent and temporary. Many Asian American minorities who behaved respectably during

Covid-19, including physicians and nurses on the front lines responding to the disease, have been racially harassed, verbally and physically.[157]

In response to anti-Asian American sentiment, former democratic presidential candidate Andrew Yang wrote an opinion article in which he advised Asian Americans to demonstrate, embrace, and showcase their American-ness by performing acts of patriotism and civic duty.[158] Yang was essentially saying that Asian Americans should respond to racism by engaging in respectability politics, which is a type of racial stereotyping—albeit a self-inflicted one—that is based on the rhetoric of the model minority myth.

In most cases, Asian Americans strongly disagreed with Yang. Three famous actors reviled Yang in tweets. George Takei, who played Mr. Sulu in the original *Star Trek* series, tweeted this viewpoint: "Yang is way off the mark here. During WWII, Japanese Americans often felt we had to prove our loyalty because of others' racism. Japanese American soldiers fought bravely and died in huge numbers for our nation. We don't have anything we need to prove."[159] In addition, Steven Yeun, who played Glenn Rhee in *The Walking Dead* tweeted, "Don't perform nationalism out of fear. Enact collectivism as human beings going through a crisis together. Rise above, educate, remain steadfast in knowing that an Asian American is part of the fabric of this nation. So help each other as you would anyhow because you're American."[160] And Simu Liu, a Chinese Canadian actor who starred in the movie *Shang-Chi and the Legend of the Ten Rings*, tweeted, "At a time when Asian diaspora from around the world are experiencing massive racism and discrimination, Andrew Yang basically just told us to suck it up, eat a cheeseburger, and buy an American flag."[161]

Opponents of respectability politics believe it is a dangerous fallacy, on three levels: logical, emotional, and spiritual. Jenn Fang, an Asian American feminist blogger and vascular developmental biologist, addressed all three in her response to Andrew Yang. First, she argued that respectability politics simply does not work as a way of stopping racism. Second, she stated that respectability politics offers its believers a false sense of security and protection. Third, she said that respectability politics perversely shifts blame and responsibility from oppressors to the oppressed. About Andrew Yang's call for Asian Americans to engage in respectability politics, Fang wrote:

> Respectability politics argues that we don't deserve the right to be protected from racism; instead, that we must earn protection from racism through good behavior. Asian American history (and indeed the history of all non-White people) teaches the error of this faulty logic time and time again. Being suitably respectable, culturally assimilated, or intellectually gifted is no protection from racism. Fred Korematsu was still jailed. Wen Ho Lee was still imprisoned. Vincent Chin was still murdered. Asian American history abounds with more examples than I can possibly list here. And yet, Yang fails to understand how racism works; or perhaps, more specifically, he fails to see racism as a

systemic problem. Yang suggests we work individually to prove ourselves loyal and friendly to the racists who would attack us. This does not challenge racism; at best, it might only temporarily deflect or delay it. It doesn't say, 'Racism is wrong' only 'Don't hurt me — I'm one of the "good ones." Hurt them.' This is model minority reasoning, miniaturized. It operates only by casting some Asian Americans as acceptably patriotic and exceptionally talented, while castigating others as disloyal and insufficiently American—and therefore more deserving of scorn, skepticism, and attack.[162]

The above quote explains why respectability politics does not work as a response to eradicate or even mitigate racism. As Fang points out, systemic racism is an institutional and structural problem requiring societal education and global changes. Asking individual minority members to change *their* behavior so as to appease racists is a local change and not a solution.

Respectability politics is akin to model minority rhetoric in several ways. First, it pits one proper subset of minorities against other proper subsets of minorities. Second, respectability politics sets a very high bar for minority behavior (like model minority behavior) that everyone must achieve in order to avoid being targeted by racist attacks. Third, respectability politics ignores the reality that racism is expressed in cultural, institutional, and social ways.[163]

Other than Andrew Yang's statements, and the tweets

in reaction to Yang, there have been several responses to anti-Asian racism, including public service announcement (PSA) videos, such as one released by the non-profit Ad Council titled, "Fight the Virus. Fight the Bias. Love Has No Labels."[164] The video features "testimonials from a firefighter, a nurse, a driver, an artist, the celebrity chef Melissa King, and others who describe being told to 'go back to China' or having people spit in their direction."[165] Emmy-winning writer Alan Yang, known for such popular shows as *Parks and Recreation* and *Master of None*, stated that anti-Asian racism "hit[s] very close to home" and "wasn't an abstract idea to me, something theoretical" because "I knew people this was happening to." As US federal leaders largely ignored the surge of anti-Asian racism accompanying the outbreak of Covid-19, "the fight against pandemic-related harassment of Asian-Americans has largely fallen to civil rights groups, marketing agencies, social media accounts and nonprofit organizations, which have promoted hashtags like #IAmNotCovid19, #RacismIsAVirus, #HealthNotHate and #MakeNoiseToday."[166]

In an informative PSA video released by the National Committee on US-China Relations, Jennifer Ho, a professor at the University of Colorado, Boulder, and Frank H. Wu, president of Queens College, CUNY, deconstructed the origins and history of the model minority stereotype. They assessed its damaging repercussions in light of Asian American activism and solidarity among all minority groups. Model minority rhetoric is a form of whitewashing and false flattery. It unsubtly criticizes every other racial minority group in America. Ho points out that to call someone a model minority "is actually inaccurate, it's very damaging, and it's definitely divisive."[167] Likewise, Frank Wu compares East Asian and Western cultures by pointing to various proverbs and sayings. First, he cites the Chinese saying, "Don't go looking for trouble" and the Japanese proverb, "The nail that sticks out gets pounded down." He then points out how those statements contrast with the way Americans are encouraged to be active in civic engagement and politically vocal.[168] In light of the American ethos, Wu urges Asians and Asian Americans "to stand up and speak out by bridge-building in coalition with others that share their ideals."[169]

To respond effectively to racism, we need to understand what motivates and fundamentally underlies racism. As stated earlier, racism is power plus prejudice; therefore, it is helpful to recognize two factors. A history of institutionalized violence, conquest, laws, and policies has enabled one group to have power over other groups. Therefore, overcoming racism requires us to change that power imbalance. Second, fear and ignorance can lead to prejudice. So, to overcome racism, we must also reduce fear and ignorance. The next chapters offer some ideas on how to do that.

Chapter 8

Overcoming Fear, Ignorance, and Prejudice

J ane Elliott famously demonstrated how easy it is for children to learn prejudice in her "blue eyes, brown eyes" learning exercise.[170] As an experiment, she taught third graders that kids "with blue eyes were better, smarter, and superior to those with brown eyes . . . and therefore they were entitled to perks, like more recess time and access to the water fountain. . . . The next day, she reversed the roles and taught that brown-eyed students were superior and therefore should receive perks."[171]

In a PBS documentary about this exercise, Elliott recalled that she "watched wonderful, thoughtful children turn into nasty, vicious, discriminating little third graders."[172] During a guest appearance on *The Tonight Show* starring Jimmy Fallon, Elliott wore a sweatshirt stating: "God created one race / THE HUMAN RACE."[173] The shirt expressed her view that overcoming prejudice requires us to recognize our common heritage.[174] "Racism is ignorance based on being miseducated. Racism is a result of being indoctrinated instead of educated," she said.[175] Elliott, along with Dr. Nathan Rutstein, a former lecturer at the University of Massachusetts Amherst School of Education, both described prejudice as "an emotional commitment to ignorance."[176] They say that racism is rooted in "the ignorance of how it feels to be discriminated against based on your race."[177] Fear plus ignorance plus low self-esteem can equal bias, bigotry, discrimination, hatred, and prejudice. Whereas fear is a biological, evolutionary reaction, ignorance and self-esteem can change endogenously. People can be educated, but they can also refuse to learn any information they do not want to learn. They can and will manipulate their personal beliefs by accepting only certain facts in order to avoid cognitive dissonance.[178] Some people tie their identities and self-worth to cherished misinformation, dearly held wrong beliefs, and partisan world views. The *raison d'être* of some cults, institutions, organizations, pandemics, panics, and religions is that some people are strongly committed to not learning about reality. Ignorance precipitates fear, which motivates ignorance—ad infinitum.

Economics of Identity

A person's identity within a cultural context can have a direct economic impact. Rachel Kranton, a professor of economics at Duke University, and George Akerlof, a Nobel Prize winner in Economics, coauthored a pioneering article titled "Economics and Identity" in which they analyze "how a person's sense of self affects economic outcomes."[179] Akerlof and Kranton developed an economic analysis of how people pursue identities that give them economic benefits while seeking to avoid costs to themselves. The article demonstrates that third parties can cause persistent changes—both beneficial and costly—to a person's or group's identity, and it emphasizes that some people have the freedom to choose their identities whereas others do not have that freedom. Akerlof and Kranton also published the book titled *Identity Politics: How Our Identities Shape Our Work, Wages, and Well-Being*. Professor Claire Hill has also published work on the law and economics of identity.[180]

All people have multiple identities that can be hidden or salient. For example, social psychological research shows that Chinese Americans have "selected individualistic (i.e., unique and noncooperative) options to a greater extent [when] the American, as opposed to [the] Chinese, identity was evoked."[181] People decide which identity to reveal or assume depending on the moment and circumstances. I often self-identify as a law and economics professor, but when asked about my race and ethnicity, I would refer to myself as a Taiwanese American, or as an Asian American— and sometimes as a carbon-based life form. However, I cannot control how people will respond to these identities. For example, someone who is angry about Covid-19 might decide to identify me as a target of their animus, disgust, or violence. In other words, we all have a self-perceived identity that may or may not be accepted by the broader society.

As with many other contested issues, racism and efforts to eliminate it evoke strong emotions, emotions that can have long-lasting and possibly irreversible consequences.[182] There can be no enforceable laws against a person's racist emotions, or even feelings of animus, but there are and can be laws against emotionally motivated violent acts. Laws, such as those pertaining to hate crimes, are difficult and costly to enforce, with no guarantee of success. And even if the law is successfully enforced, the prosecution cannot bring the dead back to life.

However, the law and other institutions can help to change people's behavior—by making racial violence more costly to the perpetrators. In so doing, the law can also effectively delegitimize morally wrong social norms and attitudes. Martin Luther King Jr., who won the 1964 Nobel Peace Prize, made this point when he said, "While the law may not change the hearts of men, it can, and it does change the habits of men. And when you begin to change the habits of men, pretty soon the attitudes will be changed; pretty soon the hearts will be changed."[183]

Legislation and enforcement could also be used to hinder *nonviolent* racism, but this would divert resources away from responses to violent racism. For this reason, we need a more decentralized, non-legalistic, and self-help way to counter the more subtle forms of racism that occur each day. One often overlooked approach is to use humor.

Utilizing Humor to Mitigate Nonviolent Racism

Humor provides a non-adversarial, nonconfrontational, and nonthreatening way to counter nonviolent racism. Morgan Spurlock, the director of the documentary film *Super Size Me,* observed that, "We have a mantra at our company, which is, 'If you can make someone laugh, you can make someone listen.'" People respond positively to humor and laughter. Behavioral research finds that humor can raise perceptions of status and hasten meaningful connections. Honest conversations about nonviolent racism can be difficult, but humor can help to lower the emotional heat. Overcoming all types of racism requires communication, compassion, empathy, kindness, and mindfulness. Humor can facilitate the communication and connection we need.

Jenny Yang (not related to Andrew), a former labor organizer who is now an actor, stand-up comedian, and writer, responded to Andrew Yang and his "respectable politics" advice to Asian Americans by creating a brilliant and hilarious video parody in which she tells her peers to proudly display their American-ness. In the video, Jenny is seen walking around Los Angeles while wearing a red top, blue jeans, white socks, white sneakers, a blue scarf, a yellow medical face mask, and white latex gloves. She introduces her video by saying, "The coronavirus has a lot of Americans scared of Asians. So, Andrew Yang says we can't make them be less racist. We just have to be more American. Let's see if that works. Come on!" She holds up a homemade sign that says, "Honk if you won't hate-crime me" and offers random passersby free Clorox wipes. Yang also hands out her nice all-American résumé with a black six-foot pole. On the streets, she shouts, "God bless the USA!" and repeatedly chants "U-S-A!" and sings, "You're a grand old flag, you're a high-flying flag" and "glory hallelujah." She reassures the people she meets that she is extremely American, proving her point by saying *woot!* and asking for ranch dressing wherever she goes.[184]

In the last minute or so of the video, also posted on Twitter, Yang captions in turquoise font that Asian Americans should study their history to better understand the connections that they have with the histories of all Americans, including those of all other ethnicities in the US. Yang urges Asian Americans to demonstrate solidarity with and support for people who suffer from bigotry, discrimination, prejudice, racism, and oppression. Everyone, she says, can fight for civil liberties, just as the African American social movements have demonstrated. She concludes by stating that we do not and should not have to prove that we are so-called "good Americans" for us to "deserve to be treated with decency and dignity."[185]

Jenny Yang complimented Andrew Yang for being honest and vulnerable when he described himself as feeling somewhat ashamed and self-conscious about being an Asian American when a frowning, middle-aged man glared at him outside a grocery store. Nonetheless, Jenny was disappointed that Andrew did not address the problem of being ashamed when he was confronted by negative anti-Asian perceptions.

Instead, he chose to double down by rejecting his Asian identity. In doing so, he implied that being American and being Asian are antithetical, and that Asian Americans were somehow not doing their best to help others.[186]

Jenny argued against the idea of respectability politics with a more sensible option, saying that if "someone is seeing your face and all they're feeling is racist anger toward you as a representative of China because they think China is the one that caused the virus, what are you going to do? Are you going to pull out your SAT score? Are you going to go, 'Look at my report card. I was a 4.5 student. Don't beat me up with your bat?'"

Her overall point, which she effectively conveys with humor and sarcasm, is true: All humans deserve to be treated with common decency and dignity. People shouldn't have to conform to respectability politics to please the majority culture or to protect themselves from racism. That's just wrong . . . and it does nothing to prevent racism.

If I were to rewrite Andrew Yang's messaging, I would say this: "It is a scary time right now, and everyone has many reasons to be scared. We shouldn't lash out against those of us who have been falsely associated with the disease, because Asians overall are not responsible for the pandemic. For all of us to be better Americans—including Asian Americans who might be facing increased anti-Asian harassment right now—we should lead by exercising a deeper level of compassion and support for each other." That's it. That's all he needed to say.

To his credit, Andrew Yang agreed with many of the

points made by Jenny Yang, Jenn Fang, and other critics of his perspective.[187] But the anger and frustration that many Asian Americans felt about his article—the strong emotions to their fears about anti-Asian American hatred—demonstrated the power of emotional contagion.

This is why the use of humor can be so helpful. Humor, parody, and satire can engage, challenge, and change people's hearts, attitudes, and behavior—in ways that the law can't. Humor and law can be used in complementary ways to overcome racism. The law is better suited to engage and mitigate *violent* racism and humor is better suited to engage and mitigate *nonviolent* racism.

Nonviolent racism, left unchecked, can and often does become violent, in part because those individuals who practice nonviolent racism develop certain behaviors and a mindset that can escalate to violence. Thus, by mitigating nonviolent racism we can also reduce violent racism. To be clear, there are certainly limits to humor's power to counter violent racism, but it can be an effective way of engaging and reducing nonviolent racism before it becomes violent.

Psychologist Gordon Allport pointed out that prejudice is a hostile attitude or feeling that has been learned. Without correction, it becomes resistant to facts, ignores honesty and truth, and leads to avoidance, discrimination, or legalized (institutionalized) racism, violence, and maybe genocide.[188] In this context, humor can engage and counteract prejudice by helping a person to become more open to changing his or her attitude. Instead of remaining in ignorance, people can come to accept a wider array of relationships and enjoy a peaceful coexistence with other groups.

There is a difference between prejudice and discrimination. Prejudice occurs when one person prejudges other people before truly understanding them. Discrimination occurs when someone acts against those people based on the preexisting prejudice. Humor, by addressing the underlying prejudice in a more palatable and less-threatening way, can therefore effectively reduce discrimination.[189]

Jennifer Aaker, a professor of business at Stanford University, and Naomi Bagdonas, a lecturer at Stanford University, wrote *Humor, Seriously* to help business professionals understand the effectiveness of humor in daily life and work. The book is based on a course they have co-taught at Stanford Graduate School of Business to hundreds of executives and MBAs. This delightful and funny book analyzes and discusses research from biology, neuroscience, psychology, leadership, and behavioral science about how humor can affect human decision-making, emotions, and motivations. The authors show that the human brain is "hardwired to respond to humor and laughter." Humor, they argue, can "increase perceptions of status, quicken the path to meaningful connection, unlock creativity, and boost resilience."[190] Humor also helps to improve trust between people and to facilitate learning.[191] Leaders can also benefit from the use of humor.[192]

An intriguing model of information acquisition and avoidance is based on the observation that information can positively and negatively change people's actions, feelings, and cognitions.[193] The model proposes that individuals evaluate information based on three values. The first relates to whether people see information as being helpful or useful for making decisions. The second value is related to the information's emotional or hedonic benefits. The third value pertains to the information's cognitive or sense-making usefulness. People often attribute a positive or negative "weight" to each value and mentally sum them up. Depending on whether the overall sum is positive or negative, they will either acquire, avoid, or be indifferent to the information. Individuals can ascribe different weights to each dimension of information value depending on how much each type of information value matters to them.

When people evaluate information about racial groups, they often place a heavy weight on negative aspects of information, especially when that information appears to threaten their identities. In addition, they tend to place less weight on information that might lead them to make behavioral or attitude changes with respect to racial groups. This means that people are often prone to distance themselves from people of a different ethnicity. However, humor can help people be more receptive to information about other ethnic groups; that is, to switch all three information values from negative to positive. Humor offers a non-adversarial, nonconfrontational, and nonthreatening way to counter and reject racism. When this occurs, people often discover their commonalities rather than their differences.

On December 15, 1984, *Saturday Night Live* presented

a skit titled "White Like Me."[194] The title was a play on a book by White journalist John Howard Griffin who in the 1950s took medication to darken his skin and wrote about his experiences while traveling in the southern states.[195] In the skit, Black comedian Eddie Murphy portrays his experiences pretending to be a White man. He hires makeup artists to apply white makeup to his face and hands, watches hours of the television show *Dynasty*, and reads countless Hallmark cards. He then becomes Mr. White and gets a free newspaper from a White shopkeeper, free drinks during a music party, and—even though he has no credit, collateral, or identification—an interest-free loan from a White banker. The skit demonstrates how skin color can change a person's experiences in daily life, and how it can affect the way others see us.

Each of us has an overall identity, but it is composed of many factors. Our professions, family backgrounds, religions, gender, nationality, culture, character, and personal tastes all play a role in making us who we are. An identity may provide comfort, a sense of belonging, and even self-understanding. However, it becomes problematic when our identities lead us to an us-versus-them mentality. Then division ensues. Unfortunately, racial identity tends to be a prominent cause of division between human beings.

To categorize each other seems to be common among humans, but these categories are inevitably reductionist, meaning that they oversimplify the vast complexity of a human into a single dimension, which removes the richness of a person's many dimensions. We are all multidimensional.

To avoid division, we should all hold our identities loosely. Two areas of psychological research support this view. The first pertains to "psychological flexibility," which is an important component of human flourishing and well-being.[196] This research, along with the practice of mindfulness, teaches us to be aware of our experiences without developing a rigid attachment to them. The second area of study relates to having an awareness of our self-complexity—the diversity of our perceived identities.[197] People who score high in self-complexity awareness are less likely to experience depression, low self-worth, mood swings, and perceived stress.[198]

By developing psychological flexibility and an awareness of our complex human experiences, people can significantly reduce racist tendencies. But there is a deeper issue involved: Our *beliefs* about the racial aspects of human beings are usually fundamentally false. We address that question in the next chapter.

Chapter 9

The Inaccuracy of Racist Beliefs

Racial beliefs are, in fact, *probability* beliefs. A person with a racist mindset makes assumptions (forms beliefs) about what a specific individual has done in the past and might to do in the present and future. For a racist, these probability beliefs are conditional only on the basis of a person's race.

An example of a stereotypical, false, and *positively* biased racial belief that exemplifies the so-called model minority myth, would be that all AANHPIs are less likely to face discrimination in the workplace than African American professionals. An example of a stereotypical, false, and *negatively* biased racial belief that exemplifies white supremacy would be the belief that all European Americans are superior to other races. A third example of a racial belief is that all races or ethnicities are worthy of dignity, love, and respect. This compassionate, empathetic, positive, and transformative racial belief is related to research by Deborah Cantrell, a University of Colorado, Boulder professor of law who explores transformative silence and protest.[199]

My point is that a person's beliefs about how others might behave in the present or future will in turn strongly influence how that person behaves. Racial probability *beliefs* often lead to racist *behaviors*. Understanding that relationship is central to reducing racism in any society.

We All Have Many Stories to Share

First, racist probability beliefs are false because they are based on a reductionist view of human beings. They assume that a person can be defined entirely by race or ethnicity when in fact every person's identity is far more diverse and complex than his or her race. We are all shaped by many experiences, not just our physical characteristics.

On an episode of Stephen Colbert's television program *The Late Show*, African American actor, comedian, writer, and producer Keegan-Michael Key compared the differences between his experiences with police before and after he became famous. Now, due to his celebrity, they see him as an individual, not as a Black adult male.[200] Key referred to a TED Talk titled "The Danger of a Single Story" by the brilliant Nigerian author Chimamanda Ngozi Adichie in which she encourages people to avoid basing their views on a single story about another individual or country.[201]

When that happens, she said, people often develop a deep misunderstanding of that individual or country. Similarly, the company P&G produced a commercial called "Widen the Screen to Widen Our View," which aimed to "share the full richness of the Black experience" and to "broaden the spectrum of the images we see, the voices we hear, the stories we tell, and the people we understand. Fully."[202]

In the United States, far too often and tragically, the only story people know is a person's skin color. The statistical inference problem of attempting to extrapolate the behavior of complex, dynamic, ever-changing, multidimensional humans from observing the single, noisy variable of skin color is that skin color is not what statisticians call a sufficient statistic. Skin color is not a sufficient factor for predicting human behavior.

Every person is like a "high-dimensional topological manifold," which refers analogously to high-dimensional Euclidean space. The topological manifold corresponding to an individual consists of that person's evolving emotional, mental, and physical attributes. It also comprises the person's life choices, beliefs, experiences, memories, personality characteristics, and potential futures. Intuitively, we know that high-dimensional human beings cannot be accurately defined by the single variable of skin color. Attempting to reduce any individual to just that physical attribute is a serious injustice and a categorical mistake. It can be mathematically proven that it is impossible to project a very high-dimensional manifold into a single number and be able to capture all the rich information content of that manifold.

Racial Beliefs and "Street Calculus"

Pulitzer Prize-winning American cartoonist Garry Trudeau is perhaps most famous for his comic strip Doonesbury, which chronicles the adventures of, among others, Michael James "Mike" Doonesbury. Trudeau's comic strip often included political and social commentary, such as a single-frame titled "Street Calculus."[203] In this one-frame scene, Trudeau presents a Black man and a White man walking toward each other on a sidewalk in the evening. Thought bubbles drawn above their heads depict their risk assessments of the other as each decides whether and how to greet the other. Race is one of their risk factors and the other is being male. The White male sees that the Black male is wearing a pair of loafers, carrying a Federal Express envelope, wearing a polo shirt, and whistling Sondheim music—all mitigating factors. The Black male observes that the White man is carrying groceries, looks to be over forty, and is humming Motown—also mitigating factors. For each of them, there are four mitigating factors and three risk factors. Hence, both males decide to politely greet each other.

Scientists who study decision-making through the lens of psychology and cognitive neuroscience have found that most people assess risks as feelings that arise during experiential, quick modes of system-one thinking. People rarely make risk assessments in a deliberative, slow mode of system-two thinking. In other words, people use "street calculus," as depicted by Trudeau, to make risk assessments.

Their racial beliefs can and usually do influence their in-the-moment decisions.

People might not take the time to do even basic street calculus. In 2019, while I was walking down a steep street in hilly San Francisco to a symposium on well-being and the practices of law, and while submerged in thought about my presentation, a man who was muttering to himself suddenly approached me and punched me in the upper thigh. I informed one of the symposium's organizers about this unexpected event later that evening and she made sure that all symposium attendees had car rides back to their hotels that night and the next. Was this incident motivated by racial hate? We will never know. But due to the stress caused by the incident, I unwittingly hurried through my presentation, speaking at a faster rate than normal. An audience member noticed and told me afterward that she wished I could have spoken at a slower pace.

Street calculus, as we can see, is an example of how racial probability beliefs are always inaccurate; they are too simplistic and narrow to encompass the manifold complexity of a human being.

"You've Got to Be Carefully Taught"

What is the origin of a person's racial beliefs? This has long been a critical and intriguing question. Possible answers include genes, evolution, parents, friends, culture, mass media, and social media. At least one film asserts that education—at home or at school—is the cause of racist beliefs. The play and film versions of *South Pacific*, written by Richard Rodgers and Oscar Hammerstein II, included six words in a song that summarize this view: "You've got to be carefully taught." Using music, the writers suggest that intolerant racial beliefs are taught and reinforced.[204] Just before the character Lieutenant Cable sings the song, he says that racism is "not born in you! It happens after you're born."[205] During a touring production of the musical in Atlanta, Georgia, legislators at the time were so offended by the song's lyrics that they introduced a bill outlawing such entertainment. Georgia State Representative David C. Jones said that any song that justifies interracial marriage covertly threatens America's way of life. Hammerstein expressed surprise that "anything kind and humane must necessarily originate in Moscow."[206] (An internet search will lead you to the complete lyrics.)

People naturally become highly attached to their beliefs, as if they were prized possessions,[207] or like protected babies.[208] There are still many debates about the origins of racial beliefs, but we know that people become very defensive if they feel those beliefs are threatened. And that is a significant problem when a person's beliefs are, in fact, racist and hateful.

Implicit Bias and Implicit Racism

Former Secretary of State Hillary Clinton pointed out the inaccuracy of racist beliefs during her first presidential debate against Donald Trump on September 26, 2016. Clinton spoke about the social psychology concept of "implicit bias" in relation to racism. "I think implicit bias is a problem for everyone, not just police," she said. "I think, unfortunately, too many of us in our great country jump to conclusions about each other. And therefore, I think we need all of us to be asking hard questions about, you know, why are we feeling this way?"[209]

Earlier, on April 20, 2016, at St. Paul's Baptist Church in Philadelphia during a roundtable about gun violence, Clinton also referred to implicit bias. "We all have implicit biases," she said. "What we need to do is be more honest about that and surface them. Because today, most people believe that they don't have those biases."[210]

There is abundant evidence that implicit bias permeates human societies.[211] With a high frequency, implicit bias shows up as "implicit racism," specifically in the form of microaggressions,[212] a word that Harvard Medical School psychiatrist Chester Pierce coined in 1970 to describe slight, subtle, frequently unintentional types of prejudice,[213] such as covertly racist expressions, everyday indignities, and understated insults.[214] Derald Wing Sue, a professor of psychology and education at Columbia University Teachers College, proposed a taxonomy of microaggressions[215] and popularized the concept and word.[216]

Not everyone agrees with the research about microaggressions. For example, Scott O. Lilienfeld, a psychology professor, criticized the psychology research literature about microaggressions, saying that it was "far too underdeveloped on the conceptual and methodological fronts to warrant real-world application." He urged "abandonment of the term 'microaggression' and . . . a moratorium on microaggression training programs."[217] Other concerns about microaggressions include the potential for exaggerating abuse, which could result in increased "victim mentality" and the triggering of possible retaliation.[218]

Edward Cantu, a law professor at the University of Missouri, Kansas City and Lee Jussim, a psychology professor at Rutgers University, have also critiqued the concept of microaggression, stating that it encourages psychological fragility, lacks scientific proof, and relies too heavily on subjective evidence.[219] Social psychologist Jonathan Haidt and best-selling author Greg Lukianoff, who is president and CEO of the Foundation for Individual Rights in Education, point out that when people avoid perceived microaggressions it limits their personal freedom and results in emotional self-harm. They add that when people rely on authority figures to call out and cancel microaggressions, it can atrophy their own ability to self-mediate disputes.[220]

This debate about microaggressions erupted at Rutgers University in 2020 when a White first-year law student quoted a racial slur from *State v. Bridges*,[221] a 1993 New

Jersey Supreme Court judicial opinion. Many Black students called for a school policy to ban the utterance of racial slurs regardless of context, and they demanded formal, public apologies from the student who quoted the slur and from the criminal law professor who allegedly acquiesced in its usage.[222] Both apologized in April 2021 during a meeting of students convened by the professor. The situation received national attention when hundreds of law school students and campus organizations across the US signed a petition in support of the Black students at Rutgers.[223]

Intense debates about microaggressions have also spilled into the workplace. Many workers have likely attended mandatory diversity training sessions about implicit bias and microaggressions. Most employers and university administrators who implement diversity training have a genuine desire to improve equity and inclusion in their organizations, but some are cynically engaging in nothing more than public relations and litigation defense strategies. Unfortunately, it is clear that most training programs, if not all, have dubious efficacy and unproven positive impacts. These educational programs, which are often heavy-handed, may provoke sustained negative impacts in the form of backlash and triggered resentment.[224] As of this writing, it is not clear what types of education efforts are effective at reducing implicit bias in corporations, universities, and other organizations.

A plethora of law professors have written many law review articles that discuss the prevalence of implicit bias in many areas, including communications law, corporate governance, criminal justice, legal education, employment anti-discrimination law, health law, housing and property law, judicial decision-making, mediation, and torts. There is significant concern about how implicit bias might affect jury selection. This concern has led several legal professional associations,[225] such as the American Bar Association,[226] the National Center for State Courts, [227] and the National Center for Juvenile Justice[228] to publish materials about implicit bias in jury selection.

In light of these debates and concerns, the main thing to remember is that the concept of implicit bias explains why there is "racism without racists."[229] Implicit bias provides a no-fault rationale for unconscious racism.[230] It is, therefore, an appealing, comforting, and polite way to discuss racism in public because it avoids the need to confront the contentious issue of explicit racism.

The problem is that common language used to discuss implicit racism can reduce our awareness about the serious impact it has on people. Michael Selmi, a law professor at Arizona State University, observed that many law professors "have fallen hard for implicit bias and dozens of articles have been written espousing the role implicit bias plays in perpetuating inequality. Within legal analysis, a common mantra has arisen that defines implicit bias as unconscious, pervasive, and uncontrollable." Selmi pointed out that "labeling nearly all contemporary discrimination as implicit and unconscious is likely to place that behavior beyond legal reach." He added that "most of what is defined as implicit bias could just as easily be defined as explicit or conscious bias." He has challenged that common narrative "by questioning the unconscious nature of implicit bias and showing that such bias is less pervasive and more controllable than typically asserted."[231] I concur with him.

Many Americans face the danger of unconscious or tacit racism.[232] We also face the related, real, and pernicious issue of explicit racism, which is far more inconvenient and uncomfortable to address than unconscious racism due to implicit bias. But the fact is that some people explicitly act on their inaccurate racial beliefs.

Explicit racism is wrong. In the coming pages I will show why this is the case and present ideas for challenging explicit racism by improving racial beliefs. I will also apply some novel economic theories about "belief-based utility." These economic theories explain how some people derive pleasure from their beliefs, even racist beliefs that inflict pain on others.[233] These theories also show how people often have a preference for social belonging with those who share their beliefs, which is tied to identity considerations.[234]

I will also describe recent interdisciplinary and multidisciplinary theories of "deliberate ignorance," which occurs when people make a conscious choice to ignore knowledge or information that counters their beliefs.[235]

Chapter 10

Why Racism Is Wrong

Is the United States a racist country? The answer to that question depends on whether we are willing to include as evidence all periods of US history or only certain periods. The answer also depends on how we define racism.[236] In the American past, the nation has engaged in the genocide of Native Americans, the enslavement of African Americans, a legal doctrine of separate but equal, the lynching of Chinese Americans, the internment of Japanese Americans, and the expulsion of Hispanic Americans. Today, the US seems to be a relatively less racist country than before, but it is far from being a post-racial, colorblind utopia,[237] as demonstrated by recent violence against AAPI populations during the Covid-19 pandemic.[238]

In terms of how we define racism, most people today (not all) agree that Americans hold implicit racial beliefs. But, as stated in the previous chapter, the focus on implicit bias provides cover, and presumably unintended safe harbor, for the old-fashioned, raging, and unfashionable racists—those who are explicitly racist.

Christopher Eisgruber, the president of Princeton University, charged his cabinet in June 2020 to develop "plans to combat systemic racism at Princeton and beyond."[239] However, according to Sergiu Klainerman, a professor of math at Princeton, the term "systemic racism" is too broad to be helpful. In his view, to say that all American institutions, including Princeton, are "structurally and systemically racist" reduces our ability to distinguish between different categories of racism and racial harms. He argues that such wording could fuel the tendency to "unearth allegedly previously hidden forms of oppression, [thereby] fomenting grievances and creating new and dangerous divisions."[240]

With so many views about how to converse about implicit and explicit racism, it can seem like we are caught in a relativist's trap: The definition of racism depends on who is doing the defining. This situation is reminiscent of a joke in which a university's staff is interviewing three candidates for its president. When the search committee asks the first finalist, who is a highly awarded mathematics professor, "What is 1+1?" she answers two and provides them with an elegant proof based on the Peano axioms. When the search committee asks the same question to the second finalist, a highly awarded physicist, she says the answer is two and provides them with experimental evidence. When the search committee asks the same question to the last finalist, a law professor, she answers, "What do you want it to be?" The staff hires the lawyer on the spot!

When the leaders of higher education institutions and prominent corporations acknowledge the existence of systemic racism in their organizations, it might seem like progress. But these declarations of guilt are often forms of public theater designed to placate angry students and maintain a positive image in the public sphere. They fail to address the genuine problems caused by explicit bias, including the harms of explicit racism. Public relations responses to racism often resemble the "voluntary" confessions of China's tortured citizens during Mao Zedong's "Great Proletarian Cultural Revolution" during which the masses were forced into reeducation (indoctrination) programs.[241]

Instead of joining the common chorus about the evils of implicit racial bias, I will instead focus on explicit racism. Specifically, I will point out the reasons why racism is undeniably wrong.

Racist Beliefs Lack Supporting Evidence

The central problem with racism is that it is based on untrue, negatively biased, subjective beliefs rather than on evidence-based, objective beliefs. The foundational tenets of racism, discussed in this book, are simply false.

Racist beliefs can be inherited from parents and family, or adopted through contact with acquaintances, friends, classmates, and colleagues. Beliefs and stereotypes can propagate from chat rooms, politicians, fake news, message boards, rumors, and social media. When people absorb and adhere to false information about people of other races, and if their unfounded assumptions are never called into question, racist falsehoods can persist across generations.

This is why education is so important. Lessons about Black, Indigenous, and people of color (BIPOC) in public schools and higher education can play a critical and patriotic role in reducing racism.[242] And because racism often spreads through relationships—virtual or physical— we could reduce false racial beliefs by encouraging positive interactions between racial groups.

Discriminatory racist beliefs might also stem from evolutionary factors. Recent research by Andrew W. Lo, a professor at MIT Sloan School of Management,[243] and Ruixun Zhang, a professor at Peking University, published in the inaugural issue of the academic journal *Collective Intelligence*, indicates that "evolutionary forces may be fueling collective tendencies to discriminate."[244] The authors present an evolutionary game-theoretic model of bias, discrimination, and political polarization due to people incorrectly attributing random adverse events to observable features unrelated with those events.[245] Negative feedback and path dependence can result in even stronger biases and levels of discrimination, which are locally evolutionarily stable strategies. Their sophisticated model demonstrates how policy interventions could nudge the "madness of mobs" toward the "wisdom of crowds" by targeted shifts in environmental factors rather than by outlawing undesirable behaviors. Policies might include "proactively providing educational, social, and economic opportunities to counteract negative feedback loops, [and] encouraging more accurate beliefs among current and future generations through early exposure." Such policies would exemplify the art and science of what Stanford Professor Geoffrey L. Cohen calls "situation-crafting." The goal is to foster an emotional sense of belonging and connection that can bridge political divides, open people up to identity-threatening information, and combat racism. (See Cohen's 2022 book *Belonging: The Science of Creating Connection and Bridging Divides*.)

My point is that false racial beliefs lead racists to think and/or act in ways that are disconnected from the objective truth about human beings. Racist beliefs are usually binary, meaning that the racist sees other people only through a lens of "us versus them." Everyone who is not "one of us" is automatically a potentially threatening "them." This reflects a strong underlying prejudice, adherence to stereotypes, or tendency to make snap judgments ("street calculus"). Racists fail to see the magnificent complexity of each person.

In addition to living with untrue perspectives, racists often demonstrate overconfidence about their racial beliefs; that is, they tend to lack humility in relation to their wrong views. They believe they are absolutely right. Economist Kenneth Arrow observed that, "Vast ills have followed a belief in certainty."[246] When a person believes unyieldingly that a race will absolutely predict another person's behavior, the racist is demonstrating a "low variance" mindset. People with low variance thinking fail to see the heterogeneity and individual differences of people within any racial group that is different than their own.

How Racists Seek to Justify Hate

Although racists usually strongly adhere to their false beliefs, they typically realize that those beliefs are at odds with basic human decency. They understand that explicit racism violates core principles of ethics, decency, fairness, justice, and morality. Therefore, an explicit racist—an individual who adheres to wrong, hate-filled, negatively biased, subjective racial beliefs—must invent justifications for his or her hateful way of life. Almost universally, racists justify their beliefs and actions by defining the targets of racism as being less than human. By devaluing the targets of hate, the racists come to see themselves as being superior, and they come to believe that the targets of racism *deserve* to be treated in subhuman ways.

This warped, deranged reasoning—that a target group of humans is subhuman—enables racists to avoid cognitive dissonance while enacting cruel, hateful actions against other human beings. The false justification allows racists to numb their consciences. It enables them to act on hate-filled beliefs and to reject the truth that all humans deserve care, compassion, empathy, kindness, love, and respect. This manufactured justification—to falsely devalue human beings—has led racists throughout history to commit innumerable atrocities.

Perhaps because of the illogical backflips required to falsely justify racism, racists are often fearful of publicly sharing their racist beliefs and actions. For example, they often communicate to each other with "dog whistles" and innuendos. Ku Klux Klan members traditionally wear hoods to hide their identities. We witnessed an effort to publicly dehumanize immigrants from Central America and Mexico when certain well-known US political leaders called them "bad hombres" and "rapists" who steal jobs from US workers—while simultaneously disavowing any racist beliefs.

Timur Kuran, an economics and political science professor at Duke University, has written extensively about people who misrepresent their true beliefs due to perceived social pressure. Kuran calls this tendency "preference falsification." The idea is that people often hide or lie about their true beliefs to maintain their position within a social context. Thus, explicit racists are likely to hide their racist views from the public, even though they might eventually commit racist acts.

Unfortunately, a racist mindset can lead the broader society to be less compassionate in response to the plight of racially targeted groups. Paul Slovic, a University of Oregon psychology professor and president of Decision Research, conducted groundbreaking research about how "psychic numbing" and related factors can reduce compassion. Slovic and his collaborators demonstrated that such biases cause human "inaction in the face of some of the world's largest humanitarian challenges, including genocide, famine, and climate change."[247]

Explicit Racism Destroys Value and Wealth

Explicit racism involves hatred of, and oppression over, at least one other racial group. Such behavior produces value for and/or increases the wealth of explicit racists at the expense of their targets. The pursuit of financial gain often motivates racists to oppress other groups. For example, American slavery provided free labor to European American slaveowners at the expense of African American slaves. Other examples include former President Trump's false claims that Mexicans are stealing American jobs,[248] or Hitler's taking "advantage of the existing prejudice that linked the Jews to monetary power and financial gain."[249] Certainly, explicit racists can, at least for a while, appropriate a larger share of a country's economic output.

Heather McGhee, board chair of Color of Change, a racial justice organization, and former president of Demos, explained the overall social costs of explicit racism in her thought-provoking book titled *The Sum of Us: What Racism Costs Everyone and How We Can Prosper.* McGhee demonstrates how racism influenced the subprime mortgage crisis of 2008. To illustrate how racism hurts us all, she writes about what happened in the 1950s when people tried to integrate public swimming pools. "Grand public pools were sumptuous emblems of common leisure in the early decades of the twentieth century, steadfastly supported by White Americans until they were told to integrate them," she writes. McGhee visited the site of one such pool in Montgomery, Alabama. It had been drained and cemented over since 1959 so that nobody could ever enjoy it again. As one reviewer of McGhee's book said, "I was reminded of the old saw about 'cutting off one's nose to spite one's face.' . . . It's a self-defeating form of exclusion, a determination not to share resources even if the ultimate result is that everyone suffers."[250]

McGhee also argues that the legacy of slavery in the United States is reflected in today's "depressed wages and scarce access to health care in the former Confederacy. But it's a blight that's no longer relegated to the region." In large part, she writes, "the story of the hollowing out of the American working class is a story of the Southern economy, with its deep legacy of exploitative labor and divide-and-conquer tactics, going national." She also realized "how most White voters weren't operating in their own rational economic self-interest" by voting for Trump in 2016 because his economic plans "promised to wreak economic, social, and environmental havoc on them along with everyone else." The author argues that "White Americans have been steeped in the [economic] notion of 'zero sum'—that any gains by another group must come at White people's expense" in such areas as our environment, health care, and voting rights. This zero-sum "cramped mentality is another legacy of slavery, . . . which really was zero sum—extractive and exploitative, like the settler colonialism that enabled it." Belief in a zero-sum world, she argues, "has always optimally benefited only the few while limiting the potential of the rest of us, and therefore the whole." Her main point is that "our fortunes are tied up with the fortunes of others.

We suffer because our society was raised deficient in social solidarity."[251]

Explicit racists will invariably and undoubtedly shrink the total size of a country's economic output. Why? For one, murder decreases the quantity and quality of labor supply. Second, to the extent that racism reduces immigration, the US loses thousands and thousands of hardworking, entrepreneurial men and women with their hardworking children. Many immigrants to the US have been pioneers in research and development in STEM fields, including the NASA moon landing program.[252] Hitler's persecution of Jews, his rejection of so-called "Jewish physics,"[253] and his multiyear "final solution" to exterminate the Jewish people through mass genocide led Albert Einstein[254] and many other Jewish and German physicists to flee Germany.[255] As a result, Hitler lost tremendous intellectual talent, leading to incalculable long-term economic losses in Germany.

Slavery exacerbates the problem of intrinsic motivation.[256] It also increases well-known principal agency problems, such as agency costs (including monitoring costs),[257] moral hazard,[258] influence costs,[259] and sabotage.[260] In short, forced labor reduces productivity, a fact backed by theoretical reasons and empirical evidence. By contrast, cooperation through free trade and voluntary labor market exchanges produce more total economic output than coercion through involuntary, forced labor. Fear motivates compliance in some people but it also motivates rebellion in other people.

Explicit Racism Is Divisive and Unsustainable

Explicit racism is, by its own definition, divisive. In the long run, such divisiveness is unsustainable because it can potentially lead to civil war, revolution, and/or uprisings. Racists divide people into an allegedly superior in-group, to which they belong, and an allegedly inferior out-group, to which the targets of racism belong. This hierarchical stratification is created and promulgated by racists to justify their hateful and subjective racial beliefs.

Racists are often unconcerned by the divisiveness of their racism, but they usually fail to see that racism is unsustainable. They desire to maintain the culture, institutions, norms, and social structures that keep them in power and give them economic advantages, but their racism plants the seeds of its own demise; a racist system is based on conflict instead of cooperation, and that leads to wealth destruction, not wealth creation. Stated in academic terms, racism leads to Pareto suboptimality not Pareto efficiency.

Although explicit racism sows its own impermanence and instability, it can persist for hundreds of years. Roman slavery lasted centuries until the Roman Empire collapsed. The eventual and inevitable disintegration of a racist system, however, does little to dissuade racists in the interim. They can be shortsighted and myopic. They can prefer to enjoy the short-term benefits of racism without thinking about how the seeds they sow will lead to future demise. This makes them less interested in changing their ways. They may want to think about what kind of society their progeny will inherit from them. If they persist in being racist overlords, their children and grandchildren could live in a world that is economically, intellectually, and socially impoverished.

Racism Is Mentally and Physically Unhealthy—Even for Racists

A large body of science-based evidence shows that victims of racism experience high levels of anxiety and stress. They also suffer with physical problems related to stress-induced, accelerated biological aging,[261] and injuries from physical violence.[262] Surprisingly, there is also science-based evidence to show that even implicit racists also suffer from mental and physical health problems.[263]

Explicit racists who live and work in large metropolitan regions in the US unavoidably and repeatedly must interact with people of different races, often in proximity. For the racist, these benign interactions take their toll over time due to ongoing chronic acute stress reactions that cause the release of stress hormones, a faster heart rate, reduced blood flow to the brain and limbs, and increased risk of high blood pressure, type 2 diabetes, and cancer.[264] In other words, racism causes self-inflicted mental and physical decline. This occurs because racists think that social interactions with their racial targets are threatening rather than opportunities for personal growth.[265] By constantly living with these perceived "threats," they experience well-known fight-or-flight physiological responses, including restrictions in blood flow and the release of the stress hormone cortisol. These biological responses interrupt digestive processes and break down muscle tissue. The muscles, including the heart, of racists can become weaker and the immune system can become damaged. In a multiracial society like the US, the racist beliefs of racists will continue to dramatically impair their mental and physical health.[266]

Researchers have found evidence of the negative physical impact of racist beliefs in three laboratory studies involving European Americans with implicit racial bias. These studies analyze implicit racism, not explicit racism because, as of this writing, there are no field or experimental studies with explicit racists. Nevertheless, the conclusions of the studies almost certainly apply to explicit racists.

One study involved European American males who interacted socially by playing the game Boggle with African American men.[267] Another study involved European Americans and Hispanic Americans who agreed to disclose personal information to each other.[268] A third study required European Americans and African Americans to perform job interview evaluations of the European Americans.[269] In these studies, the European Americans with stronger implicit racism experienced higher levels of distress, as measured by autonomic nervous system responses, cortisol levels in saliva samples, and levels of dehydroepiandrosterone sulfate (DHEA-S), a hormone that helps repair tissue damage caused by overtaxing the fight-or-flight physiological response.[270]

In all three studies, European Americans who were less implicitly racist experienced very different physiological responses to interracial social interactions. European Americans who had positive attitudes toward individuals of different races enjoyed adaptive, happy, and healthy responses during interracial interactions. The studies also found that people can learn to have positive implicit racial attitudes. In the second study above, researchers found that implicitly prejudiced European Americans had lower cortisol levels after they completed friendship-building tasks with individuals of a different race over several weeks. The same study also found that European Americans who had made a cross-race friend during the research process went on to seek more interracial relationships.[271]

Many people do things that are unhealthy for them in the long run, such as bad eating habits and sedentary lifestyles, simply because they enjoy the short-term benefits. The same occurs with racists. In fact, some people can become *addicted* to explicit racism.

All said, racist beliefs are clearly false. They lack logic and objective evidence, and they result in widespread, long-term, economic, social, national, and physical harm—including to the racists.

Chapter 11

Beliefs and Behavior

In the previous chapter, I pointed out how racism is based on false beliefs that devalue human beings, which leads to numerous negative outcomes, including for racists. Because racism is rooted in untrue beliefs, we can learn how to disrupt it by looking at what researchers have found about how beliefs affect behavior. That's what this chapter is about.

The study of beliefs is often related to statistical decision theory,[272] which is canonical in economics and other fields such as clinical medicine, engineering, finance, management, and public policy.[273] This theory helps explain how our beliefs influence our decisions, how we assess information, and how those assessments influence the probability of acting on our beliefs.[274]

Economists also study what people assume about other people's internally driven actions. Multiperson decision theory, also known as game theory, helps us study the economic and social interactions in which individuals make choices that impact others. Within game theory, researchers have demonstrated the link between a person's beliefs and the probability of how those beliefs might influence behavior in relation to various sets of information. Game theory also accounts for arbitrarily small perturbations of beliefs and for how those might affect a person's behavioral strategies.

Psychological game theory (PGT) offers a mathematical language to study how beliefs affect people's motivations. This area of game theory enables researchers to incorporate emotions, fairness, image concerns, reciprocity, and self-esteem into economic analysis.[275] For example, a law-related example of PGT might show how anger and surprise affect decisions about filing a lawsuit, agreeing to a settlement, or going to trial.[276] Another PGT example analyzes the role of embarrassment, guilt, and remorse in maintaining informal social norms.[277] PGT models can even help us understand the role of emotions and beliefs in leadership.[278]

In this chapter, I refer to economic theories of "belief-based utility" and "deliberate ignorance." These theories, which are novel and transformative, represent significant departures from traditional research about beliefs and behavior. This branch of exciting research appreciates that people's minds enjoy or dislike certain beliefs and information. Depending on the mind's preference, an individual will be more likely or less likely to engage with various beliefs and information. For example, some people will avoid information about a potential illness because they fear it might be bad news. Likewise, some people will avoid information that might debunk their false racial beliefs.

Pleasures and Pains from Beliefs

Nobel Prize-winning economist Thomas C. Schelling, a game theorist, once stated "that, as consumers, we live in our minds."[279] We experience both positive and negative emotions based on what we believe to be true. This also applies to racial beliefs. Schelling says that:

> Things that make me happy or unhappy, at any level of consciousness that I can observe, are the things that I believe and am aware of. . . . An unavoidable question is whether I could be happier if only I could believe things more favorable, more complimentary, more in line with my hopes and wishes, than what I believe to be true. That might be done by coming to believe things that are contrary to what I know, such as that my health and reputation is better than it is, my financial prospects or my children's prospects [are] better than they are, and that I have performed ably and bravely on those occasions when I did not, or it might be accomplished by improving the mix of my beliefs by dropping out—forgetting—some of the things that cause me guilt, grief, remorse, and anxiety. Whether I would be happier, whether my welfare should be deemed greater, with those improved beliefs is one of the questions. Another is whether, if I had the choice, I would elect a change in my beliefs. . . . A third question is whether you would encourage me to manipulate my beliefs in the interests of my happiness or permit me to if you had anything to say about it.[280]

Schelling describes the human mind as a "consuming organ, the generator of direct consumer satisfaction."[281] What we choose to believe or disbelieve about other racial groups is often influenced by a desire to preserve positive emotions and to avoid cognitive dissonance.[282]

Andras Molnar, a researcher at the University of Chicago Booth School of Business, is helping to lead the resurgence of interest in research about beliefs. Molnar's website summarizes the importance of this trend: "Most of the things that affect our welfare happen in our minds. We dwell on successes and failures, the past and the future, relationships, fears, regrets, disappointments and triumphs, whether we have fulfilled our goals, and whether other people like and respect us."[283] He has studied why people care about what other people believe, and how our beliefs about ourselves affect our own well-being and actions. Molnar has also looked at what drives people to seek and disclose information.[284] These questions are central to the way that racial beliefs influence behavior.

People often intentionally refuse to consider information that might upset their beliefs. In the fascinating book titled *Deliberate Ignorance: Choosing Not to Know*, a group of economists, historians, computer scientists, legal scholars, philosophers, psychologists, and sociologists consider why some people prefer to avoid information and attainable knowledge about important issues, which they call deliberate ignorance.[285] These researchers formally model the underlying motives for deliberate ignorance, including the refusal to accept negative facts about one's own racial group.[286]

Fostering Accurate Beliefs

Robert Wright, in his book *The Moral Animal*, described how a person will defend strongly held beliefs even if the beliefs are false or lack evidence.

> The proposition here is that the human brain is, in large part, a machine for winning arguments, a machine for convincing others that its owner is in the right—and thus a machine for convincing its owner of the same thing. The brain is like a good lawyer: Given any set of interests to defend, it sets about convincing the world of their moral and logical worth, regardless of whether they in fact have any of either. Like a lawyer, the human brain wants victory, not truth; and, like a lawyer, it is sometimes more admirable for skill than for virtue.[287]

The human brain is like a zealous but possibly ethically compromised attorney.[288] Our brains are heavily invested in keeping our attitudes and maintaining our beliefs. Because people can directly experience pleasures and pains from their own beliefs and the beliefs of other people, they often choose to strongly defend inaccurate beliefs and to ignore information that might debunk those falsehoods.

This raises the question of whether we should try to convince people to change their beliefs, and if so, how to do that. Can legal rules and institutions change idiosyncratic beliefs if people do not want to change? Do people have a fundamental right to choose deliberate ignorance? Or do people in a democratic society have a fundamental social right and perhaps responsibility to require their fellow citizens to abandon beliefs that might lead to hate crimes, refusal to comply with public health initiatives, or even an insurrection?

Researchers have shown that various institutions and legal doctrines can discourage or encourage deliberate ignorance. For example, Eyal Zamir and Roi Yair emphasize some possible legal methods to overcome deliberate ignorance.[289] They suggest the idea of mandating that people learn important information, making it so conspicuous that it is hard to ignore.

In May 2021, the National Museum of American History, the Asian Pacific American Center, and the American Association of Retired Persons (AARP) cosponsored an online event to commemorate Asian Pacific American Heritage Month. The event featured an online screening of a program titled "We Are American and We Stand Together: Asian American Resilience and Belonging." Near the conclusion of this presentation, Lonnie G. Bunch III, the secretary of the Smithsonian Institution, said, "The unvarnished truth about our history is often hard to hear, but it is also the best way to understand and to heal." He added that, "We believe that knowledge is the best antidote to ignorance and fear."[290] I agree also with Kenneth Arrow, who said, "Knowledge is a free good. The biggest cost in its transmission is not in the production or distribution of knowledge, but in its assimilation. This is something that all teachers know."[291]

During the program described above, CeFaan Kim, a reporter for WABC-TV in New York, spoke with Ronny Chieng, a Malaysian actor and comedian. Chieng expressed his optimism that laws and institutions could help people change their false racial beliefs.

"I think there is a lot of freedom to tell these stories [in the US]," he said. "There are lots of organizations and there are leaders who care. They're providing legal help. There are some people who will escort your elder relatives to where they need to go. There's assemblymen and women who care and who are there. And if you find them, you will be inspired by these leaders who are actually there to provide help to the community."[292]

All racism is rooted in beliefs. By understanding why people choose and defend their beliefs—even when they are false and destructive—we can find better ways to disrupt racism. In the next chapter, I address legal and economic factors that can help us bring about a less racist culture.

Chapter 12

The Law and Economics of Hate and Racism

Hate and racism are rooted in false racial beliefs, and these beliefs can play a role in shaping our legal and economic framework. A legal and economic system can support or suppress racism. Depending on the characteristics of that framework, racism will either flourish or wither. So, we need legislation that bans and punishes hate crimes, and we need a market that refuses to provide financial rewards for racist actors.

Economics of Hate

Elizabeth M. Wheaton, a lecturer in economics at Southern Methodist University, in her book *The Economics of Human Rights* (2019), writes that "hate is at the root of human rights violations."[293] She uses microeconomic theory to analyze issues such as violence against women, asylum seeking, terrorism, child abuse, genocide, capital punishment, and hate.[294] By integrating economics and human rights, she has been able to foster novel solutions for important social problems. Each chapter of her book describes the economic benefits and costs of a particular human rights issue, and it offers ideas for preventing human rights violations. [295]

Wheaton defines hate as, "An intense hostility and aversion usually deriving from fear, anger, or sense of injury."[296] She points out that neuroscience researchers have found distinct neural correlates of hate, demonstrating "that there is a unique pattern of activity in the brain in the context of hate."[297] Her conclusion is that hate imposes many costs but offers few benefits.[298] Unsurprisingly, haters benefit (sometimes economically) while imposing costs on the hated. Hate also uses up scarce resources that could have been employed in more productive endeavors.

The amount of research literature about the economics of hate and its related negative emotions,[299] such as envy, is small.[300] However, many prominent researchers have addressed this matter. Gary Becker, who won the 1992 Nobel Prize for Economic Sciences, analyzed envy among siblings.[301] He later formed the basis of a 2002 econometric analysis of empirical hate crime data.[302] Another researcher, Edward Glaeser, a professor of economics at Harvard, developed a political-economic model of the interactions between hate-driven voters and politicians who foment hate by repeating false narratives about an out-group.[303]

Glaeser found that such politicians are motivated to start and spread hate-creating stories to discredit opponents whose policies benefit the out-group. For example, egalitarian, progressive politicians might foment hatred against wealthy minorities, and politicians opposed to economic redistribution might manufacture hatred against poverty-stricken minorities. For hate to endure, voters must accept hate-creating stories. Therefore, if they had legal or financial incentives to learn the truth and change their beliefs, the motivations to foment hate would falter. Glaeser's model explains how the hatred of Blacks evolved in the southern region of the US, how hate repeatedly fueled anti-Semitic episodes in Europe, and how anti-Americanism increased in Arab countries. Glaser's model also provides an eerily prophetic explanation for former President Trump's anti-Mexican and AAPI hate rhetoric.[304]

I focus next on legal approaches to disrupt racism.

Hate Crime Laws

The legal definition of a hate crime is related to negative bias toward a specific group. The word *hate* in "hate crime" does not refer to the emotions of anger, rage, or loathing. Instead, *hate* refers to bias against individuals and groups who have characteristics protected by federal or state legislation, such as color, race, national origin, gender, gender identity, sexual orientation, disability, and religion.[305]

A hate crime usually involves violence, such as arson, assault, murder, vandalism, or even the *threat* to commit such acts. It might also include a conspiracy to commit such crimes, even if unsuccessful. In addition to hate crimes, there are also hate *incidents*, which are discriminatory or prejudicial acts that do not meet the legal standard of a crime. Hate, by itself, is not a crime.[306]

Legislation designed to deter hate crimes typically involves the application of penalties that are more severe than corresponding non-hate crimes.[307] Hate crime laws do not punish individuals for holding unobservable hateful thoughts; instead, they punish individuals for choosing hateful reasons to commit acts already deemed to be criminal.[308]

A primary public policy justification for hate crime legislation is to reduce the likelihood of retaliatory crimes. An example of retaliation occurred in 1992 in Los Angeles after African American motorist Rodney King was severely beaten by White police officers. When all the officers were acquitted, riots erupted in the city and protesters severely beat a White truck driver in retaliation.[309]

In the US, federal statutes against hate crimes are also called bias crimes.[310] The most well-known federal hate crime law is The Matthew Shepard and James Byrd Jr. Hate Crimes Prevention Act.[311] This 2009 law expanded the federal definition of hate crimes, expanded federal prosecutors' available legal toolkits, and enhanced federal law enforcement ability to assist state and local law enforcement partners. The law eliminated previous jurisdictional hurdles to prosecuting certain acts of violence motivated by race and religion, and it enacted additional federal protections against the targets of hate crimes.

In April 2021, the US Senate voted ninety-four to one to pass the Covid-19 Hate Crimes Act, which was designed to bolster and expedite the review of Covid-19 related hate crimes, particularly crimes against AAPIs.[312] (The lone opposing vote was cast by Republican Senator Josh Hawley of Missouri who argued "that it mandated an overly expansive collection of data around hate crimes that could slide into government overreach."[313]) The bill also aimed at expanding channels to report hate crimes and establishing a series of public education campaigns about bias against people of Asian descent. The bill then went to the US House of Representatives, where it passed, despite sixty-two opposing votes by Republicans. President Biden signed the bill into law on May 20, 2021.[314] At the White House signing ceremony, Biden said, "All of this hate hides in plain sight. . . . Too often it is met with silence—silence by the media, silence by our politics, and silence by our history. . . . We simply haven't seen this kind of bipartisanship for much too long in America. . . . My message to all of you who are hurting us is, we see you, . . . And the Congress has said, 'We see you.' And we are committed to stopping the hatred and the bias. . . . Of all the good that law can do, we have to change our hearts. We have to change the hearts of the American people. I mean this from the bottom of my heart. Hate can be given no safe harbor in America." Vice President Kamala Harris said, "This bill brings us one step closer to stopping hate, not just against Asian-Americans, but for all Americans. . . . Racism exists in America," she said. "Xenophobia exists in America. Anti-Semitism, Islamophobia, homophobia, transphobia, it all exists." Biden also called for an end to the "ugly poison" of hate, adding that, "I believe with every fiber of my being that there are simple core values and beliefs that should bring us together as Americans. One of them is standing against hate. . . . Every time we're silent, every time we let hate flourish, you make a lie of who we are as a nation."[315]

As a result of legislation, the US Department of Justice and the Federal Bureau of Investigation, in addition to campus security authorities, are required to collect and publish hate crime statistics.[316] Forty-seven states and the District of Columbia have hate crime laws and/or require the collection of hate crime data.[317] Arkansas, South Carolina, and Wyoming do not have hate crime laws or data collection requirements.[318] The Department of Justice provides an interactive online map that people can use to learn about hate crimes and view case examples about each state.[319]

The US Supreme Court held unanimously that enhanced penalties for racially motivated crimes do not violate criminal defendants' free speech rights, because such laws do not punish an individual for exercising their freedom of expression.[320] It should be no surprise that crime is not protected by the First Amendment.[321] Penalty-enhancement hate crime laws permit courts to consider a criminal's motives during sentencing. This judicial opinion paved the way for states to pass hate crime laws that consider whether a crime was committed or initially contemplated because of an intended victim's status in some protected class.[322] In an earlier landmark case of *Chaplinsky v. New Hampshire*,[323] the Supreme Court articulated the "fighting words" doctrine, a limitation of the First Amendment's guarantee of freedom of speech by defining "fighting words" as "those which by their very utterance inflict injury or tend to incite an immediate breach of the peace."[324]

A significant discrepancy, known as the "hate crimes reporting gap," exists between actual versus reported hate crimes. Targets of hate crimes often do not file a report because of several understandable reasons: limitations with the English language, fear of retaliation, mistrust of law enforcement, and personal feelings of embarrassment and shame. These barriers are unfortunate, because reporting hate crimes to law enforcement agencies can provide victims with help. Reporting such crimes also sends a strong public message to potential hate crime perpetrators that target communities will not tolerate hate crimes. In addition, accurate hate crime reporting permits communities and law enforcement agencies to comprehend the scope of hate crimes within a community, which improves law enforcements' ability to identify and prevent violent attacks predicated on hate.[325]

Active, lively debates remain over how well hate crime laws deter these crimes.[326] Supporters of the laws believe that hate crimes harm not only the target(s), but also people within the entire specified protected class. By this argument, hate crimes have widespread, devastating, and long-term impacts on families, communities, and possibly an entire nation.

However, there are critics of hate crime laws. They often question whether these laws do more harm than good. Dan Kahan, a law professor at Yale, argues that some individuals so highly value their group identities that they *perceive* attacks against their group as being worse than other crimes.[327] In other words, the gravity of a hate crime is related to a group's *reaction* to it, not to the nature of the crime itself.[328]

Heidi Hurd and Michael Moore, both law professors and legal philosophers at the University of Illinois, argue that hate crime laws do not prove that: (1) hate is a morally worse motivation for criminal activity than other motivations for crime, such as greed, jealousy, sadism, or vengeance; or that (2) bias and hate are uniquely more responsive to criminal sanctions compared to other possible motivations for crime.[329] Hurd and Moore also believe that whether one type of criminal motivation is morally worse than another depends on the specific facts of each case in question; therefore, they say it is flawed to claim that some motivations for committing a crime are morally worse than other motivations.

According to Hurd, hate crime laws require governments to promote a specific type of moral character for its citizenry, which she says exemplifies the perspective that installing virtue and eliminating vice are legitimate state objectives. Hurd says this contradicts principles of liberalism.[330] She also claims that enhancing punishments for hate-motivated offenses implies that criminal justice systems are treating the same crimes with different standards, which she believes contradicts the basis of criminal justice.

Enforcement of hate crime laws depends on prosecutorial discretion. Proving the hate component of these crimes is often difficult, particularly in cases involving AAPIs.[331] The difficulty stems from the fact that hate against AAPIs often intersects with other forms of bias, including sexism and classism.[332] Obviously, racial and non-racial motivations for crimes are not mutually exclusive; both racial and non-racial motivations for a crime may coexist.

Earlier I wrote about the horrific 2021 spa shootings in Atlanta, which killed eight people, including six Asian American women.[333] That tragedy exemplifies the intersectionality of AAPI hate and sexism. The police and some media outlets were reluctant to categorize the murders as hate crimes because the gunman claimed to be motivated by sex addiction.[334] However, the Korean media immediately categorized the murders as hate crimes, in part because eyewitnesses heard the shooter say, "I'm going to kill all Asians," and because all four Korean females were in the age range of fifty to seventy, and because three women at the location did not even give massages.[335]

In response to this case, Fani Willis, the district attorney of Fulton County, which includes Atlanta, announced in May 2021 that her office would seek hate-crime charges and the death penalty.[336] Willis also stated "that she believes her office will be the first to use Georgia's new law on bigoted attacks and that her charging decisions 'send a message that everyone within this community is valued.'"[337] Georgia hate crime law "mandates that Georgians convicted of felony hate crimes have at least two years added to their sentence."[338] Georgia passed the hate crime law in the summer of 2020 after outrage over a graphic video of two White men chasing and shooting dead Ahmaud Arbery, an African American age twenty-five,[339] while he jogged near his house.[340]

Georgia enacted hate crime legislation after the state's Supreme Court struck down, in 2004, its previous hate crime statute,[341] which the court said was unconstitutionally vague.[342] That statute defined hate so broadly that, as Justice Carol Hunstein wrote,[343] a "rabid sports fan convicted of uttering terroristic threats to a victim selected for wearing a competing team's baseball cap; a campaign worker convicted of trespassing for defacing a political opponent's yard signs; a performance car fanatic convicted of stealing a Ferrari" could have qualified to invoke the hate crimes law.

From a legal and economics perspective, the penalty enhancements of hate crime statutes run into an "upper bound" problem; that is, once a crime has the death penalty, there is no additional deterrence possible. This means that a person who commits a hate crime with the death penalty attached to it will not be deterred from committing more crimes to avoid capture. Regardless of your personal ethical and moral attitudes about capital punishment, there is a problem here: Once a criminal has committed a crime meriting the death penalty, that criminal is in effect incentivized to commit more crimes because there can be no worse punishment. It is as if the criminal has entered a zone where additional crimes are penalty free. This is well-known as the "deterrence problem" of capital punishment.

The Economics of Explicit Racism

In addition to legal perspectives, it is possible to view explicit racism as a commodity, something that certain people want to consume and that other people are happy to supply. This perspective will undoubtedly seem strange to anyone who is not an economist. After all, economists are trained to see everything through the lens of economics.[344] Still, it is true that there are quasi-markets for the sale and purchase of hate, bias, and racism. In these markets, there are suppliers and consumers of racism, and there are those who "boycott" (resist) racism.

William J. Baumol and other economists developed an economic theory known as "contestable markets." First, contestable markets have weak or no barriers to entry, and they have no exit barriers. Second, this type of market does not require sunk costs that cannot be recovered. Third, contestable markets comprise incumbents who have no technological advantage over new entrants. Under these conditions, we can come to at least two conclusions. First, new entrants force incumbents to compete. Second, new entrants force incumbents to focus more on maximizing sales—to grab market share—than on profits.[345]

In light of these conclusions, we can ask whether the contestable markets theory applies to quasi-markets for explicit racism. Consider first that those who "supply" explicit racism fall into three categories: the *producers* who provide narratives about explicit racism; the *enablers* who provide the racist ideologies and mindsets; and the *investors* who facilitate racism for personal economic or political benefits.

Robert Shiller, who won the 2013 Nobel Prize in Economics, created a new field of study known as narrative economics, which is "the study of the spread and dynamics of popular narratives." He looks at how stories, particularly those of human interest and emotion, change through time and affect economic fluctuations.[346] These stories, if they go viral, can influence markets. Examples include narratives that technology stock prices never fall, that housing prices can only rise, or that some firms, such as banks, are too big to fail. Another narrative is that stock markets are democratized for all investors.[347] We saw this play out when a group of small investors used the social network Reddit to coordinate the purchase of GameStop, AMC, and Nokia stock to cause losses for hedge-fund short sellers.[348] Shiller pointed out that a market narrative should be seen as nothing more than "a song, joke, theory, explanation, or plan that has emotional resonance and that can easily be conveyed in casual conversation."[349]

The idea of a powerful narrative or story can also lead

to large changes in racial beliefs. Historically, hateful racist beliefs have been motivated and justified by a compelling and easy-to-spread tale about how a certain race of people can cause economic woes or public health ills. For example, Hitler's promotion of the "master race" falsehood used Jewish people as scapegoats for Germany's problems. More recently, Trump consciously used rhetoric about Mexicans being "bad hombres," and about the "Chinese virus," the "Wuhan virus," or the "kung flu" to spread hate, fear, and anger.[350]

As stated above, there are consumers who demand explicit racism and derive pleasure from holding racist beliefs.[351] Some people are addicted to explicit racism. And there are those who benefit, economically or otherwise, from racism.

Thankfully, in the "market" for racism, there are those who resist it. Some are actual or potential targets who, by their mere existence and resilience, resist the racists. Others challenge the ideologies and mindsets that underlie racism. Others disrupt racism by disputing false racist narratives with truth-based narratives.

Racists should not be allowed to benefit financially or otherwise from hate. Both legal and economic measures can be applied to disrupt racism.

Chapter 13

Resistance Is *Not* Futile

I stand in solidarity with the United Federation of Planets (henceforth the Federation) in its strong opposition to a well-known phrase by the Borg in the *Star Trek* series: "Resistance is futile." The Borg, partly artificial and partly organic, seek to assimilate all other species into their collective. They always broadcast the same threatening mantra each time they encounter non-Borgs: "We are the Borg. Lower your shields and surrender your ships. We will add your biological and technological distinctiveness to our own. Your culture will adapt to service us. Resistance is futile." In the *Star Trek* series, the Borg appear in twenty-one episodes to terrorize the Federation.

Well, when it comes to the Borg—and racism—resistance is *not* futile. I believe there are three evidence-based, actionable strategies that can help us effectively resist racism, including AAPI hate: positive racial education and mindfulness; positive racial conversations and communication; and positive associations, cultures, and norms. Along with these interventions, the law can play a helpful role.

I am certainly not the first person to offer suggestions for resisting racism. Many academic studies in psychology have suggested methods for reducing prejudice. Between 2007 and 2019, researchers produced 309 manuscripts involving 418 quantitatively assessed experiments about approaches to reduce prejudice. They aimed to determine which approaches were most successful and why. Among all this work, there are some landmark studies. These landmark studies often showed that efforts to reduce racism had limited effects. This suggests the necessity for additional theoretical research about other types of psychological or structural interventions. It is fair to say that much of the existing research is neither theoretically nor empirically ready to offer actionable, evidence-based policy recommendations designed to reduce prejudice. [352]

In the meantime, I suggest three possible ways to resist racial hate. Each of my suggested interventions is inspired by evidence-based research. My hope is that these ideas will spur additional theoretical, empirical, and experimental research about the efficacy, interactions, and sustainability of these tools. In the remainder of this chapter, I address each: education, communication, and associations.

Positive Racial Education and Mindfulness

Explicit racism can only persist if people never learn the truth about the value of human beings. Racists must remain ignorant of the truth. One way to remain ignorant is to avoid all information and experiences that would disconfirm racist beliefs. Ignorance precipitates fear, and fear motivates hate. Thus, to overcome hate and racism, we need to reduce fear, anger, and ignorance.

For this reason, the first intervention is to *mandate* positive racial education and mindfulness in schools, starting in kindergarten and lasting through twelfth grade. Instruction about mindfulness would include the teaching of happiness as a skill that can be learned. I realize that teaching mindfulness could be controversial in a school setting; after all, many people think that teaching yoga and mindfulness is like teaching a religion.[353] The second intervention would be to encourage people of different ethnic groups to have positive, civil conversations. And a third intervention would be to facilitate positive mental associations, or perspectives, about races other than one's own. When people see the positive aspects of racial groups, it fosters healthy interactions among them.

The phrase "positive education" means "education for both traditional skills and for happiness."[354] This approach to education is about more than passing along information to students. It is also about helping students experience more happiness, an effort that is based on the belief that

165

happiness is a skill that all people can and should learn. We know that people experience happiness when their lives have a positive influence, when they have a cognitive sense of life satisfaction or well-being (eudaemonia), and a sense of meaning in life.

It should be clear that holding onto hate, explicit bias, and explicit racism is incompatible with living a well-lived life or attaining true happiness. To live daily with a fuming, hate-filled, and raging racism eventually leads racists to a negative self-image and sadness.

Positive racial education also includes teaching students about the positive contributions that members of *all races* have made to the arts, culture, economy, science, and technology. By including education about all races, we can hopefully avoid racial contentiousness and political controversies. There have been too many cases in which certain groups have sought to block education about, for example, African American history.[355] In many states, some activists have mistakenly conflated African American history and Critical Race Theory.[356]

The reason that I argue for the inclusion of mindfulness meditation in anti-racism education is because experimental research has found that this practice can reduce racially discriminatory behavior.[357] Positive mindfulness in education efforts can therefore reduce human suffering and increase human flourishing. It is what some scholars call "right mindfulness" versus "wrong mindfulness."[358] An example of wrong mindfulness is when a sniper lies in wait with the wrongful intent to kill. An illustration of right mindfulness is that of someone focusing on how to help others overcome suffering and achieve happiness in life. The concept of positive mindfulness is thus ethically based; it is not agnostic about moral right and wrong.

One type of positive mindfulness is called loving-kindness mindfulness (LKM).[359] "LKM meditation is a way to practice the good habits of caring, compassion, kindness, inclusion, and tolerance—instead of animus, bias, discrimination, intolerance, and prejudice."[360]

All of this can and should be part of our education systems in the US.

Positive Racial Communications

Alison Wood Brooks, the O'Brien associate professor of business administration at Harvard Business School, coined the phrase "talk gooder" to describe positive racial communication. Brooks researches the newly emerging science of conversation. She also teaches a fascinating elective course titled "How to Talk Gooder in Business and Life," an experiential course designed to help MBA students refine four conversational skills: topic selection, asking questions, levity, and kindness (TALK). *Topic selection* entails learning how "to prepare, select, shift, change, and end topics effectively." *Asking questions* involves learning how "to ask (and answer) questions well." *Levity* involves learning how "to create and appreciate moments of humor, playfulness, jackassery and joy." *Kindness* is about learning how "to speak respectfully, listen responsively, and engage receptively with opposing views."[361]

Brooks and her coauthors recently introduced a conceptual model they call the "conversational circumplex."[362] Their framework helps people have more successful conversations by identifying and understanding the participants' motives by looking at two factors: information and relations. A motivation that is strongly skewed toward only transmitting information could lead to a less relational outcome, and vice versa. By focusing on the relational as opposed to only informational aspects of conversation, we can improve the outcomes of our interactions.

The academic phrase "positive communication" originated with Julien Mirivel, professor of applied communication at the University of Arkansas, Little Rock.[363] Mirivel offers six keys to positive communication.[364] The first is to "greet to create human contact." The second is to "ask to discover the unknown." The third is to "compliment to affect people's sense of self." The fourth is to "disclose to deepen relationships." The fifth is to "encourage to give support." And the sixth is to "listen to transcend differences."

Mirivel believes that human communication can be more than the mere transmission of information. It also has the potential to be transformative, to create healthy experiences and build relationships, and to open opportunities to "learn from a position of humility and curiosity." Positive communication can help us practice what humanistic psychologist Carl Rogers defines as "unconditional positive regard: a way of looking at people with warmth, without any conditions."

By seeking meaningful opportunities for positive interracial communication—in schools, universities, workplaces, and neighborhoods—we can effectively reduce racism.

Positive Racial Associations, Cultures, and Norms

When people see the best in other racial groups— positive racial associations—they experience more compassion, empathy, love, kindness, and understanding toward each other. By contrast, anger, fear, and hate toward other groups lead to negative relational outcomes. Societies can and should instill social norms that include positive racial associations.

To replace negative racial associations based on hatred and scapegoating with positive associations based on courtesy and respect, we can create situations in which people of differing races interact cooperatively and positively to help each other achieve shared, common goals (e.g., partnerships). If such real-world opportunities are scarce, they can always occur in multiplayer video games and role-playing simulations. For example, the fictional holodeck technology featured significantly in several *Star Trek: The Next Generation* episodes is an example of a sophisticated virtual-reality simulation. Something like this could be used to educate people about how racism feels to those who are oppressed by it. Participants would assume the roles of avatars from another race while experiencing simulated forms of racism.

Academic, business, political, social, and spiritual leaders who exemplify positive racial associations can support and sustain healthy organizational cultures based on positive racial norms. One example can be seen in the way that President Biden improved the tone of US culture when he offered heartfelt speeches about stopping AAPI hate! In essence, he disrupted the former president's negative racial associations by promoting positive associations.

Getting to Know Each Other

The positive interventions mentioned above share a common intention: to encourage us to learn more about people within other racial groups—beyond their skin color. A person's skin color is determined by melanin, which occurs in different ratios.[365] The belief that skin color is the basis of a person's life story is obviously false. We know that people with the same skin color are heterogenous, with many individual differences, faiths, perspectives, and stories. It bears remembering that "to make a better world, we need to focus on what unites us, not what makes us different. After all, skin color really is only skin deep!"[366]

Dr. Martin Luther King Jr. said in a speech at Cornell College, on October 15, 1962, "I'm convinced that men hate each other because they fear each other. They fear each other because they don't know each other, and they don't know each other because they don't communicate with each other, and they don't communicate with each other because they are separated from each other."[367]

It is important to realize the idea of race itself can be understood as an artificial, historically contingent, and man-made political and social construction. Race is not a natural, objective, scientifically based genetic concept. From the social constructivist perspective, "to which most (but not all) academics and judges say they subscribe,"[368] race "cannot refer to an attribute, a genetically produced trait, or a signifier—level of melanin in skin, phenotype, distinctive names or speech—that people just have and thereby obviously belong to a designated racial group."[369] Instead, race "references a complexly constituted social fact, whereby material and dignitary opportunities are organized such that certain physical and cultural signifiers become the salient markers of consequential cultural categories, and those categories are constituted by a constellation of social relations and meanings with a definite content and organization."[370]

The social constructivist view of race suggests that race is not an exogenously fixed attribute or dimension of an individual. As Yale Professor Issa Kohler-Hausmann notes about Eddie Murphy's character Mr. White, the very notion of "'White' is essentially a metonym for a constellation of social meanings produced through a complex history of slavery, immigration, and countless other forces, not a melanin deficit (or white face makeup in his case)."[371] So, we should perceive and model race as a constellation, or in financial parlance, a "portfolio," or in mathematical terms, a "vector" of component attributes. Thus, when our perspective (point of view) changes, we begin to see the rest of the world in new ways.

Therefore, we can challenge racial hate by reducing anxiety, fear, greed, and deliberate ignorance. Research in behavioral economics and other behavioral sciences demonstrates that we can help people change their racist beliefs by helping them to become more *willing* to change.[372] We can do this based on evidence-based, optimistic knowledge related to human neuroplasticity. Individuals who have learned to possess hateful, negatively biased racial beliefs can unlearn these false beliefs and learn instead to be compassionate and empathetic toward other groups of people. This can be accomplished through positive racial education and mindfulness, positive racial communications, and by establishing positive associations, cultures, and social norms.

All these interventions can be supported by the law. Frank Wu observed that "legal change is necessary, not sufficient."[373] In other words, the law can foster, encourage, and incentivize the effort to help change people's racial beliefs in a positive direction; that is, to change people's hearts and minds about race.

Humans all too easily form tribes of in-groups versus out-groups, or haves versus have-nots. People create false divisions based on skin color, class, socioeconomic status, age, weight, sexual orientation, education, disabilities, and anything else! Nevertheless, this tendency can be countered with legal policies that support the interventions described above.

Concluding Thoughts

Anti-racism and racism are belief systems and ideologies.[374] People often treat their beliefs like possessions, something they own and from which they derive benefits.[375] This tendency among humans has been cited for hundreds of years, including by Jeremy Bentham and Adam Smith.[376]

More recent work by two behavioral economists, Andras Molnar and George Loewenstein, highlights a number of constraints on people's belief selection and revision.[377] As legal scholar and cultural cognition scholar Dan Kahan reminds us, people have preferences to share the beliefs of others in their social circles.[378] In addition to such interpersonal constraints on belief selection and revision as belief homophily and belief consonance,[379] there also are intrapersonal constraints on belief selection and revision, such as loss aversion, psychological attachment, the sunk cost effect, intertemporal consistency, and status quo preference. Quitting anything can be difficult, including racism.[380] All these constraints imply the path-dependence of beliefs and failures to ignore past beliefs. Finally, and relatedly, ideologies are indivisible sense-making narratives.[381]

Thus, anti-racism and racism are both like financial portfolios. People may find it costly to "sell" related ideas and belief systems to "buy" new ones. Nevertheless, I believe that by using the relational, economic, and legal tools at our disposal, and with persistence and time, we can disrupt racism and make our culture more inclusive and collaborative.

In this book, I have recommended the development of five policies to lower the costs of adopting anti-racist beliefs. First, utilize humor. Second, nudge the "madness of mobs" toward the "wisdom of crowds" by implementing targeted shifts in environmental factors. Doing so will be more effective than only outlawing racist behaviors. Third, teach mindfulness and positive racial education. Fourth, foster positive interracial communications. Fifth, encourage positive racial associations, cultures, and norms. Collectively, these strategies can help us defuse racial anxiety, hate, and suspicion. They can build racial camaraderie, goodwill, and trust.

It is my hope that we can live according to the good, old-fashioned American belief that a nation of people united can accomplish amazing achievements, such as landing people on the moon and bringing them back safely. The US moon landing is often hailed as proof that Americans can do anything if we put our minds to it. That technological feat obviously required many individuals to believe that the task could be accomplished.

Perhaps Americans and their elected leaders should proclaim a national goal to overcome racial hate in the next decade. Imagine what we could accomplish if we committed sufficient resources to fund policies that fostered positive racial education and mindfulness, positive racial conversations and communications, and positive racial associations and norms. It is my sincere hope that we "make it so," as Captain Picard said in many episodes of *Star Trek: The Next Generation*. I hope we will leave a less polarized and more united country for the next generation of Americans.

Many Americans today are less hopeful and more cynical. They are fatigued by Covid-19, the relentless polarization of American politics, and the seeming national acquiescence that American life will always be filled with anger, hate, and violence. That type of fatalism leads us to avoid a critical question: What kind of legacy are we leaving our children and grandchildren?

We can and must do better for our kids, nieces, and nephews. The word *harambee* in Swahili means "stronger together, mutual responsibility." It is the official motto of Kenya, as displayed on the country's coat of arms. The divisiveness of "us versus them" will not solve global climate catastrophe and many other challenges the human species faces. Instead, the unity of "us *and* them" is imperative to solving collective problems and mitigating negative externalities. Humans must learn to work together or fail apart. We must learn that our differences do not make society weaker, but instead strengthen it.

Conflicts between groups can lead us down a path of mutual destruction. We must break the age-old cycles of hate and violence that occupy much of human history. If we do not learn to live together in peace and harmony, then we will not survive ourselves. Although some conflict is inevitable, hate and violence are not. We can resolve conflicts harmoniously and sustainably. It is not helpful to blame others and point fingers, but it is helpful to praise others and lend a hand. This is not about holding hands and singing "Kumbaya," but the only way to solve the many challenges we face is to collaborate, communicate, and cooperate. It will require positive communication, trust, and mutual reliance.

~

Change often begins in our own hearts and minds. So, writing as an uncle would, I conclude the book with some gentle advice. Learn happiness and joy. Learn mindfulness, both inner and outer. Learn that you are loved and valued. Learn flexibility, grit, and resilience. Learn humility, awe, and wonder. Learn patience, empathy, and kindness. Learn compassion for others and self-compassion. Learn to treat everyone with respect, courtesy, and curiosity.

Learn personal financial literacy. Learn to be mentally, emotionally, and physically healthy. Learn to love and be loved. Learn to laugh at yourself, the human condition, and the things that happen on this pale blue dot in space. See the humor in life and enjoy it.

Acknowledgements

Writing a book is like raising a child because it takes a village. Thanks to my life partner for her advice, companionship, and love. Thanks to "Waipo," also known as my maternal grandma, for helping to raise me as a more thoughtful and mindful human being than I otherwise would have become. I am thankful to my parents who brought me into this world and raised me. Thanks especially to my mother, who worked so very hard to be the best mother she could be. Thanks to my brothers for sharing their childhoods with me, and for their fellowship as adults. Thanks to many aunts, uncles, and cousins for their diversity. Thanks to my Aunt Helen, also known as Ce-E-Ma, for her understanding. Thanks to all my nieces and nephews equally for just being themselves and for being unending sources of joy. Thanks to Aunt Margaret, a bilingual educator who exemplified happiness through mindfulness, and who passed away far too soon. Thanks to her daughter and my cousin Sherry for her helpful comments and suggestions on several earlier drafts of this book.

I am also grateful to my teachers, who include

former academic coauthors and colleagues. My eighth-grade mathematics teacher, undergraduate senior thesis advisor, and PhD dissertation advisor were all great role models. Thanks to Ho-Mou Wu for his friendship, advice, precautionary eating companionship, and work as a coauthor.

Thanks to Nancy Levit and Nathalie Martin for their advice about writing books. Thanks to Jennifer Ho, Jennifer Lee, Max Stearns, the Maryland Carey Law Virtual Constitutional Law and Economics Workshop, Jane Thompson, and Frank Wu for their helpful discussions. Kathy Stanchi offered detailed comments and clarifying feedback on an early draft of a related law review article about explicit racism. My gratitude goes to Jim Chen and Fred Tung for sharing their experiences as Asian American law professors.

Debra Austin offered invaluable friendship and partnership, as did Corie Rosen Felder, who also shared a mutual interest in legal zombification and who was a fun office neighbor. Thanks to Rebecca Huss for her friendship and support. Noshua Watson held me accountable to stay on schedule while writing this book and was an exemplary autodidact. Thanks to Olivia Ash for her example of being an entrepreneur.

Thanks to Faye Deal for being a source of sage advice. Thanks to Dr. Kathy Wu for conversations about burnout, stress, and trauma. Cassidy Erickson reminded me about nonlinear dynamical systems with positive and negative feedback loops. Thanks to Glenn McMahan for his editing and encouragement. Thanks to Dr. Michelle Ecker for her practical discussions and insights about making healthier behavioral and lifestyle changes. Dr. Rowena McBeath provided insights about empathy, life, and the importance of always asking why. Thanks to former Penn law student and current CEO of ePrep, Karl Schellscheidt, for his friendship. Karl made suggested edits, big and small. Thanks to Haley Kostic for her marketing advice. Doris Cheung provided IT support and friendship.

I'm grateful for Liz Hill and Jen Sullivan for helping to ensure that my last summer research stipend was revised to be equal to other faculty stipends. Amanda Rochette's discussions with me about health and life were edifying. Faculty coordinators Chemaine Chandler and Kathryn Yazgulian, assistant manager of faculty support Kelly Ilseng, and manager of faculty support Nicole Drane provided significant technical support.

Thanks to the following law reviews for providing me permissions to include adaptations of my previously published work in this book: *British Journal of American Legal Studies; William & Mary Journal of Race, Gender, and Social Justice; Florida International University Law Review; Northwestern Journal of Law and Social Policy; Southern California Review of Law and Social Justice; Stanford Journal of Law, Business & Finance;* and *Emory Corporate Governance and Accountability Review.*

About the Author

Peter Huang graduated in three years at age seventeen from Princeton University and was a university scholar in mathematics and economics. He quickly went on to earn a doctorate in applied mathematics (mathematical economics) from Harvard University. His principal PhD thesis advisor was 1972 Nobel Prize-winning economist Kenneth Joseph Arrow. Peter completed a JD with distinction from Stanford University Law School, where he was a Stanford Center on Conflict and Negotiation Fellow and a John M. Olin Fellow in Law and Economics.

Dr. Huang was a staff economist in the Division of Consumer Protection in the Bureau of Economics of the

Federal Trade Commission. He has published sixty-eight articles in economics journals, along with book chapters and law review articles. His recent work has been on topics related to anti-discrimination, leadership, stakeholder capitalism, and social justice. He is a frequent guest on legal and education podcasts where he talks about such topics as how the pandemic changed our personal and professional lives, mental health, the "zombification" of law students and lawyers, and the "bamboo ceiling" that Asian American law students and lawyers often face in the legal profession.

Endnotes

1   Peter H. Huang, "Structural Stability of Financial and Accounting Signaling Equilibria," *Research in Finance* 9, (1991): 37-47.

2   Daniel Eisenberg, et al., Healthy Minds Network, "The Healthy Minds Study: Fall 2020 Data Report," Fall 2020, https://healthymindsnetwork.org/wp-content/uploads/2021/02/HMS-Fall-2020-National-Data-Report.pdf.

3   Debra Cassens Weiss, "11% of Law Students Had Suicidal Thoughts in the Past Year, Survey Finds; What Can Law Schools Do?" *American Bar Association Journal,* (July 14, 2022), https://www.abajournal.com/web/article/11-of-law-students-had-suicidal-thoughts-in-the-past-year-survey-finds-what-can-law-schools-do; David Jaffe, Katherine Bender, and Jerome M. Organ, "It is Okay to Not Be Okay: The 2021 Survey of Law Student Well-Being," *University of Louisville Law Review* 60, no. 3, (2022): 439, 467, https://uofllawreview.org/online-edition.

4   Constance Wu, *Making a Scene*, (New York: Scribner, 2022).

5   Juliana Kim, "Constance Wu's Reveal Speaks to the Profound Pressure Asian American Women Face," National Public Radio, July 18, 2022, https://www.npr.org/2022/07/18/1112055817/constance-wu-asian-american-women.

6   Constance Wu, Twitter, July 14, 2022, https://twitter.com/ConstanceWu/status/1547661204545359877/.

7   Manya Koetse, "Chinese Reporter Who Cried on Air over Abe's Death Attempted Suicide after Online Backlash," What's on Weibo, July 21, 2022, https://www.whatsonweibo.com/chinese-reporter-who-cried-on-air-over-abes-death-attempted-suicide-after-online-backlash/.

8   Manya Koetse, Twitter, July 8, 2022, https://twitter.com/manyapan/status/1545386635008921600.

9   John M. Gottman et al., *The Mathematics of Marriage: Dynamic Nonlinear Models,* (Bradford, 2005).

10   Gary Chapman, *The 5 Love Languages: The Secret to Love that Lasts*, (Northfield Publishing, 2015).

11   Jerker Denrell, "The Hot Stove Effect," https://sites.google.com/site/jerkerdenrell/hot-stove-effect.

12   Mark Twain, *Following the Equator: A Journey Around the World,* (Public Domain, 1897), https://www.gutenberg.org/files/2895/2895-h/2895-h.htm.

13   Twain.

14   Kathy Wu, "Assume Every Child Has PTSD These Days Until Proven Otherwise," MedPage Today, May 28, 2022.

15   Leon Glass, "A Topological Theorem for Nonlinear Dynamics in Chemical and Ecological Networks," *Proceedings of the National Academy of Sciences* 72, (1975): 2856-2857.

16   Graciela Chichilnisky, "Sex and the Ivy League," in *Reflections of Eminent Economists*, eds. Michael Szenberg and Lall Ramrattan, (Edward Elgar Publishers: 2004), p. 108.

17   Martin Luther King Jr., Speech at Western Michigan University, December 18, 1963, https://libguides.wmich.edu/mlkatwmu/speech.

18   Kenneth J. Arrow, *The Economics of Information,* volume 4, (Belknap Press, 1984).

19   Kenneth J. Arrow, *The Limits of Organization*, (W.W. Norton: 1974).

20   Kenneth J. Arrow, "Some Mathematical Models of Race in the Labor Market," in *Racial Discrimination on Economic Life*, ed. A. H. Pascal, (Lexington Books: 1972), p. 187; Kenneth J. Arrow, "Theory of Discrimination," in *Discrimination in Labor Markets*, eds. Orley Aschenfelter and Albert Rees, (Princeton University Press: 1973), p. 3.

21   Kenneth J. Arrow, "What Has Economics to Say About Racial Discrimination?" *Journal of Economic Perspectives,* (Spring 1998): 91. See also Steven A. Ramirez, "What We Teach When We Teach About Race: The Problem of Law and Pseudo-Economics," *Journal of Legal Education* 54, (2004): 365.

22   Justin T. Huang, Masha Krupenkin, David Rothschild, and Julia Lee Cunningham, "The Cost of Anti-Asian Racism During the COVID-19 Pandemic," *Nature Human Behavior,* (2023), https://doi.org/10.1038/s41562-022-01493-6.

23   Yao Lu, Neeraj Kaushal, Xiaoning Huang, and S. Michael Gaddis, "Priming Covid-19 Salience Increases Prejudice and Discriminatory Intent Against Asians and Hispanics," *Proceedings of the National Academy of Sciences* 118, (2021): e2105125118. See also Jonathan Kahn, *Race on the Brain: What Implicit Racism Gets Wrong About the Struggle for Racial Justice,* (Columbia University Press, 2017).

24   Rachel Redhouse, "Sizzler Promotional Commercial 1991," YouTube, https://youtu.be/E3YGtQ40Qvs.

25   CNN, *Parts Unknown*, YouTube, https://youtu.be/ylKr3KQVyp8.

26   Peter Coy, "Why So Many Children of Immigrants Rise to the Top," *The New York Times,* July 11, 2022, https://www.nytimes.com/interactive/2022/07/11/opinion/immigrants-success-america.html.

27   Kelly Simpson, "Chinese Americans: Remembering a Golden Legacy," KCET, January 24, 2012, https://www.kcet.org/history-society/chinese-americans-remembering-a-golden-legacy.

28   Gordon H. Chang and Shelley Fisher Fishkin, "Geography of Chinese Workers Building the Transcontinental Railroad," Chinese Railroad Workers in North America Project, Stanford University, 2018, https://web.stanford.edu/group/chineserailroad/cgi-bin/website/virtual/.

29   George Kraus, "Chinese Laborers and the Construction of the Central Pacific," *Utah Historical Quarterly* 37, (1969): 41-42.

30   William Wei, "The Chinese-American Experience: An Introduction," *Harper's Weekly,* https://immigrants.harpweek.com/ChineseAmericans/1Introduction/BillWeiIntro.htm.

31   Chinese Exclusion Act, Pub. L. No. 47-126, 126, 22 Stat. 58 (1882).

32   George Anthony Peffer, "Forbidden Families: Emigration
      Experiences of Chinese Women Under the Page Law, 1875-1882,"
      Journal of American Ethnic History 28, (1986): 6.

33   Beth Lew-Williams, *The Chinese Must Go: Violence, Exclusion,
      and the Making of the Alien in America*, (Cambridge: Harvard
      University Press, 2021).

34   Steven Heller, "The Artistic History of American Anti-Asian
      Racism," *The Atlantic,* February 20, 2014, https://www.theatlantic.
      com/entertainment/archive/2014/02/the-artistic-history-of-
      american-anti-asian-racism/283962/.

35   Gregory B. Lee, "Dirty, Diseased and Demented: The Irish, the
      Chinese, and Racist Representation," *Journal of Global Cultural
      Studies* 31, no. 5, (2017): 6.

36   Jeff Yang, "A New Virus Stirs Up Ancient Hatred," CNN, January
      30, 2020, https://www.cnn.com/2020/01/30/opinions/wuhan-
      coronavirus-is-fueling-racism-xenophobia-yang/index.html.

37   Kelly Wallace, "Forgotten Los Angeles History: The Chinese
      Massacre of 1871," Los Angeles Public Library, May 19, 2017,
      https://www.lapl.org/collections-resources/blogs/lapl/chinese-
      massacre-1871.

38   Yang.

39   Crystal Tang, "Unpacking the Model Minority Myth," Beneficial
      State Foundation, June 4, 2019, https://beneficialstate.org/
      perspectives/unpacking-the-model-minority-myth/.

40   Kat Chow, "If We Called Ourselves Yellow," NPR: Code
      Switch, September 27, 2018, https://www.npr.org/sections/
      codeswitch/2018/09/27/647989652/if-we-called-ourselves-yellow.

41   Magnuson Act, Pub. L. No. 78-199, 57 Stat. 600 (1943).

42   Ellen D. Wu, "Asian Americans and the 'Model Minority' Myth,"
      Los Angeles Times, January 23, 2014, https://www.latimes.com/
      opinion/op-ed/la-oe-0123-wu-chua-model-minority-chinese-
      20140123-story.html.

43   Robert G. Lee, "The Cold War Origins of the Model Minority
      Myth," in *Asian American Studies Now: A Critical Reader,* eds. Jean
      Yu-wen Shen Wu and Thomas C. Chen, (Rutgers University Press,
      2010), p. 256.

44   Ellen D. Wu, *The Color of Success: Asian Americans and the Origins of the Model Minority,* (Princeton: Princeton University Press, 2015); see also Jeff Guo, "The Real Reasons the U.S. Became Less Racist Toward Asian Americans," *The Washington Post,* November 29, 2016, https://www.washingtonpost.com/news/wonk/wp/2016/11/29/the-real-reason-americans-stopped-spitting-on-asian-americans-and-started-praising-them/.

45   Jennifer Lee and Min Zhou, *The Asian American Achievement Paradox,* (Russell Sage Foundation, 2015).

46   Viet Thanh Nguyen, "Asian Americans Are Still Caught in the Trap of the 'Model Minority' Stereotype. And It Creates Inequality for All," *Time,* June 25, 2020, https://time.com/5859206/anti-asian-racism-america/.

47   Nancy Leong, "The Misuse of Asian Americans in the Affirmative Action Debate," *University of California Los Angeles Law Review,* May 23, 2016, https://www.uclalawreview.org/misuse-asian-americans-affirmative-action-debate/.

48   Nancy Leong, "Racial Capitalism," *Harvard University Law Review* 126, (2013): 2151-2226, https://harvardlawreview.org/2013/06/racial-capitalism/.

49   Nancy Leong, *Identity Capitalists: The Powerful Insiders Who Exploit Diversity to Maintain Inequality,* (Stanford University Press, 2021).

50   Gil Asakawa, "Jeff Yang in WSJ Deconstructs 'Model Minority' and 'New Jews' Stereotypes of Asian Americans," Nikkei View: The Asian American Blog, October 30, 2012, https://nikkeiview.com/blog/2012/10/jeff-yang-in-wsj-deconstructs-model-minority-new-jews-stereotypes-asian-americans.

51   Eileen Rivers and Thuan Le Elston, "AAPI Pride: Asian and Pacific Islander Heritage Helps Lift America to What It Must Be," *USA Today,* May 17, 2021, https://news.yahoo.com/aapi-pride-asian-pacific-islander-130016737.html.

52   White House, "A Proclamation on Asian American and Native Hawaiian / Pacific Islander Heritage Month, 2021," April 30, 2021, https://www.whitehouse.gov/briefing-room/presidential-actions/2021/04/30/a-proclamation-on-asian-american-and-native-hawaiian-pacific-islander-heritage-month-2021/.

53   Paula Yoo, *From A Whisper to A Rallying Cry: The Killing of Vincent Chin and the Trial That Galvanized the Asian American Movement,* (Norton Young Readers, 2021).

54   Frank H. Wu, "Asian Americans and the Future of Civil Rights," Society of American Law Teachers, webinar, May 25, 2021, https://www.saltlaw.org/video-now-available-asian-americans-and-the-future-of-civil-rights/.

55   Frank H. Wu, "Why Vincent Chin Matters," *The New York Times,* June 22, 2012, https://www.nytimes.com/2012/06/23/opinion/why-vincent-chin-matters.html.

56   Louise Hung, "35 Years After Vincent Chin's Brutal Murder, Nothing Has Changed," *Global Comment,* June 28, 2017, https://globalcomment.com/35-years-vincent-chins-brutal-murder-nothing-changed/.

57   Hung.

58   Judith Cummings, "Detroit Asian-Americans Protest Lenient Penalties for Murder," *The New York Times,* April 26, 1983, https://www.nytimes.com/1983/04/26/us/detroit-asian-americans-protest-lenient-penalties-for-murder.html.

59   Hung, 54.

60   Hung, 101.

61   Becky Little, "How the 1982 Murder of Vincent Chin Ignited a Push for Asian American Rights," *History Stories,* History Channel, May 5, 2020, https://www.history.com/news/vincent-chin-murder-asian-american-rights.

62   Little.

63   Frank Wu, 52.

64   Frank Wu, 99.

65   Gabriel Frimodig, "Fear Leads to Anger, Anger Leads to Hate, Hate to Suffering," YouTube, July 15, 2020, https://www.youtube.com/watch?v=kFnFr-DOPf8.

66   Kyle Hill, "Was Yoda's Advice Any Good Psychologically?" *Discover,* May 6, 2014, https://www.discovermagazine.com/the-sciences/was-yodas-advice-any-good-psychologically.

67   Anti-Defamation League, "Reports of Anti-Asian Assaults, Harassment and Hate Crimes Rise as Coronavirus Spreads," *American Defamation League Blog*, July 18, 2020, https://www.adl.org/blog/reports-of-anti-asian-assaults-harassment-and-hate-crimes-rise-as-coronavirus-spreads; Evan Gerstmann, "Irony: Hate Crimes Surge Against Asian Americans While They Are on the Front Lines Fighting Covid-19," *Forbes,* April 4, 2020, https://www.forbes.com/sites/evangerstmann/2020/04/04/irony-hate-crimes-surge-against-asian-americans-while-they-are-on-the-front-lines-fighting-covid-19/#7963c8a03b70; Cathy Park Hong, "The Slur I Never Expected to Hear in 2020," *The New York Times,* April 12, 2020, https://www.nytimes.com/2020/04/12/magazine/asian-american-discrimination-coronavirus.html; Sheng Peng, "Smashed Windows and Racist Graffiti: Vandals Target Asian Americans Amid Coronavirus," *NBC News,* April 10, 2020, https://www.nbcnews.com/news/asian-america/smashed-windows-racist-graffiti-vandals-target-asian-americans-amid-coronavirus-n1180556; Melody Zhang, "Don't Overlook the Virulence of Racism Toward Asian Americans," *Sojourners*, March 26, 2020, https://sojo.net/articles/don-t-overlook-virulence-racism-toward-asian-americans.

68   Sabrina Tavernise and Richard A. Oppel Jr., "Spit On, Yelled At, Attacked: Chinese-Americans Fear for Their Safety," *The New York Times,* March 23, 2021, https://www.nytimes.com/2020/03/23/us/chinese-coronavirus-racist-attacks.html.

69   Catie Edmondson, "Asian-American Lawmakers Call Out Racist Language: 'I Am Not a Virus,'" *The New York Times,* March 18, 2021, https://www.nytimes.com/2021/03/18/us/politics/asian-politicians-racism.html.

70   Kurt Bardella, "'China Virus' Redux: For Trump and Republicans, It's Open Season on Asian Americans Like Me," *USA Today,* March 17, 2021, https://www.usatoday.com/story/opinion/2021/03/04/covid-racism-asian-americans-trump-provocations-column/6904348002/; Stacy Torres, "Violence and Hate Against Asian Americans is a Health and Safety Crisis for Everyone," *USA Today,* March 18, 2021, https://www.freep.com/story/opinion/2021/03/17/anti-asian-violence-covid-safety-crisis-hurts-everyone-column/4736733001/.

71   Justin Baragona, "Trump Addresses 'Kung-Flu' Remark, Says Asian-Americans Agree '100 Percent' with Him Using 'Chinese Virus,'" *Daily Beast,* March 18, 2020, https://www.thedailybeast.com/trump-addresses-kung-flu-remark-says-asian-americans-agree-100-with-him-using-chinese-virus; Max Cohen, "Kellyanne

Conway Reacts to Trump's Use of 'Kung Flu,' Months After Calling Term 'Highly Offensive,'" *Politico,* June 24, 2020, https://www.politico.com/news/2020/06/24/kellyanne-conway-trump-kung-flu-coronavirus-337682; Andrew Restuccia, "White House Defends Trump Comments on 'Kung Flu,' Coronavirus Testing," *The Wall Street Journal,* June 22, 2020, https://www.wsj.com/articles/white-house-defends-trump-comments-on-kung-flu-coronavirus-testing-11592867688.

72   Howell Raines, "George Wallace, Segregation Symbol, Dies at 79," *The New York Times,* September 14, 1998, https://www.nytimes.com/1998/09/14/us/george-wallace-segregation-symbol-dies-at-79.html.

73   Peter Baker, "A Half-Century After Wallace, Trump Echoes the Politics of Division," *The New York Times,* July 30, 2020, https://www.nytimes.com/2020/07/30/us/politics/trump-wallace.html.

74   Gerstmann, 65.

75   Ed Park, "Confronting Anti-Asian Discrimination During the Coronavirus Crisis," *The New Yorker,* March 17, 2020, https://www.newyorker.com/culture/culture-desk/confronting-anti-asian-discrimination-during-the-coronavirus-crisis.

76   Caitlin Yoshiko Kandil, "Asian Americans Report Over 650 Racist Acts Over Last Week, New Data Says," *NBC News,* March 26, 2020, https://www.nbcnews.com/news/asian-america/asian-americans-report-nearly-500-racist-acts-over-last-week-n1169821.

77   Editorial Staff, "Hate Crimes Against Asian Americans Are at an 'Alarming Level,' UN Says," NextShark, October 20, 2020, https://nextshark.com/un-experts-trump-attacks-against-asian-americans/; Josh Margolin, "FBI Warns of Potential Surge in Hate Crimes Against Asian Americans Amid Coronavirus," *ABC News,* March 27, 2020, https://abcnews.go.com/US/fbi-warns-potential-surge-hate-crimes-asian-americans/story?id=69831920; Kristine Phillips, "'We Just Want to be Safe': Hate Crimes, Harassment of Asian Americans Rise Amid Coronavirus Pandemic," *USA Today,* May 21, 2020, https://www.usatoday.com/story/news/politics/2020/05/20/coronavirus-hate-crimes-against-asian-americans-continue-rise/5212123002/.

78   Kristine Phillips, "'They Look at Me and Think I'm Some Kind of Virus': What It's Like to be Asian During the Coronavirus Pandemic," *USA Today,* March 28, 2020, https://www.usatoday.

com/story/news/nation/2020/03/28/coronavirus-racism-asian-americans-report-fear-harassment-violence/2903745001/.

79   Dawn Kopecki, "WHO Officials Warn US President Trump Against Calling Coronavirus 'the Chinese Virus,'" CNBC, March 18, 2020, https://www.cnbc.com/2020/03/18/who-officials-warn-us-president-trump-against-calling-coronavirus-the-chinese-virus.html.

80   World Health Organization, "WHO Issues Best Practices for Naming New Human Infectious Diseases," May 8, 2015, https://www.who.int/news/item/08-05-2015-who-issues-best-practices-for-naming-new-human-infectious-diseases; Kai Kupferschmidt, "Discovered a Disease? WHO Has New Rules for Avoiding Offensive Names," *Science Insider,* May 11, 2015, https://www.sciencemag.org/news/2015/05/discovered-disease-who-has-new-rules-avoiding-offensive-names.

81   Morgan Gstalter, "WHO Official Warns Against Calling It 'Chinese Virus,' Says 'There's No Blame in This.'" *The Hill,* March 19, 2020, https://thehill.com/homenews/administration/488479-who-official-warns-against-calling-it-chinese-virus-says-there-is-no.

82   Charlotte Gibson, "UCLA's Natalie Chou Won't Stand for Anti-Asian Racism Related to Coronavirus," *ESPN,* March 26, 2020, https://www.espn.com/espnw/voices/story/_/id/28955666/ucla-natalie-chou-stand-anti-asian-racism-related-coronavirus; Natalie Chou, Twitter, March 21, 2020, https://twitter.com/NatalieChou1/status/1241478192176738304.

83   Yulin Hswen et al., "Association of '#covid19' Versus '#chinesevirus' with Anti-Asian Sentiments on Twitter: March 9–23, 2020," *American Journal of Public Health* 111, no. 5, (2021): 956; see also Elizabeth Weise, "Anti-Asian Hashtags Soared After Donald Trump First Tied Covid-19 to China on Twitter, Study Shows," *USA Today,* March 18, 2021, https://www.usatoday.com/story/news/nation/2021/03/18/anti-asian-hashtags-donald-trump-covid-19-tweet-study/4728444001/.

84   Fatemeh Tahmasbi et al., "'Go Eat a Bat, Chang!': On the Emergence of Sinophobic Behavior on Web Communities in the Face of Covid-19," Cornell University, *ArXiv,* March 3, 2021, https://arxiv.org/abs/2004.04046; see also Craig Timberg and Allyson Chiu, "As the Coronavirus Spreads, So Does Online Racism Targeting Asians, New Research Shows," *The Washington Post,* April 8, 2020, https://www.washingtonpost.

com/technology/2020/04/08/coronavirus-spreads-so-does-online-racism-targeting-asians-new-research-shows/.

85   Mark Schaller and Steven L. Neuberg, "Danger, Disease, and the Nature of Prejudice(s)," *Advances in Experimental Social Psychology* 46, no. 1, (2012): 2.

86   Stefanie K. Johnson, "Is Covid-19 Increasing Racially Motivated Crimes?" *Psychology Today,* May 22, 2020, https://www.psychologytoday.com/us/blog/stand-out-and-fit-in/202005/is-covid-19-increasing-racially-motivated-crimes.

87   Schaller and Neuberg.

88   Kenneth Letendre et al., "Does Infectious Disease Cause Global Variation in the Frequency of Intrastate Armed Conflict and Civil War?" *Biological Review* 85, no. 3, (2010): 669.

89   Kimmy Yam, "There Were 3,800 Anti-Asian Racist Incidents, Mostly Against Women, in Past Year," *NBC News,* March 16, 2021, https://www.nbcnews.com/news/asian-america/there-were-3-800-anti-asian-racist-incidents-mostly-against-n1261257.

90   Cady Lang, "Hate Crimes Against Asian Americans Are on the Rise. Many Say More Policing Isn't the Answer," *Time,* February 18, 2021, https://time.com/5938482/asian-american-attacks/.

91   Jessica Chia, "Keys, Wallet, Pepper Spray: The New Reality for Asian-Americans," *The New York Times,* May 20, 2021, https://www.nytimes.com/2021/05/20/nyregion/asian-americans-attacks-nyc.html.

92   Alexandra E. Petri, "To Combat Anti-Asian Attacks, New Yorkers Join Neighborhood Watch Patrols," *The New York Times,* April 8, 2021, https://www.nytimes.com/2021/04/08/nyregion/anti-asian-violence-neighborhood-watch.html.

93   Weiyi Cai et al., "Swelling Anti-Asian Violence: Who Is Being Attacked Where," *The New York Times,* April 3, 2021, https://www.nytimes.com/interactive/2021/04/03/us/anti-asian-attacks.html.

94   Regina Kim, "Atlanta Spa Shootings: What Korean-Language Media Told Us That the Mainstream Media Didn't," *Rolling Stone,* March 31, 2021, https://www.rollingstone.com/culture/culture-news/atlanta-shootings-what-korean-language-media-told-us-that-the-mainstream-media-didnt-1149698/.

95   Michael R. Sisak and Karen Matthews, "Video Shows Vicious Attack of Asian American Woman in NYC," *Associated Press News,* March 30, 2021, https://apnews.com/article/65-year-old-asian-woman-assaulted-nyc-street-692b82db37efae29d12e7fa638eb2e 1d.

96   Rachel Treisman, "Attack on Asian Woman in Manhattan, as Bystanders Watched, To Be Probed as Hate Crime," NPR, March 30, 2021, https://www.npr.org/2021/03/30/982745950/attack-on-asian-woman-in-manhattan-as-bystanders-watched-to-be-probed-as-hate-cr.

97   Neil Vigdor, "Attack on Asian Woman in Midtown Prompts Another Hate Crime Investigation," *The New York Times,* March 31, 2021, https://www.nytimes.com/2021/03/30/nyregion/attack-asian-woman-midtown.html.

98   American Broadcasting Company, "Search Continues in Brutal Manhattan Attack on Asian Woman Heading to Church," Channel 7, New York, March 30, 2021, https://abc7ny.com/search-continues-in-brutal-nyc-attack-on-asian-woman-heading-to-church/10459000/; Ryan W. Miller, "'Absolutely Disgusting and Outrageous': Elderly Asian American Woman Released from New York Hospital After Brutal Attack; Suspect Sought," *USA Today,* March 30, 2021, https://www.usatoday.com/story/news/nation/2021/03/30/nypd-asian-american-woman-assaulted/7057944002/.

99   Miller.

100   Nicole Hong et al., "Brutal Attack on Filipino Woman Sparks Outrage: 'Everybody Is on Edge,'" *The New York Times,* April 6, 2021, https://www.nytimes.com/2021/03/30/nyregion/asian-attack-nyc.html.

101   Vanessa Hua, "In a Role Reversal, Asian-Americans Aim to Protect Their Parents from Hate," *The New York Times,* March 29, 2021, https://www.nytimes.com/2021/03/26/well/family/asian-american-hate-racism.html.

102   Heidi Shin, "I'm Helping My Korean-American Daughter Embrace Her Identity to Counter Racism," *The New York Times,* March 19, 2021, https://www.nytimes.com/2021/03/19/well/family/Talking-to-children-anti-Asian-bias.html.

103   Massachusetts General Hospital Center for Cross-Cultural Student Emotional Wellness, "Guide for Parents of Asian/Asian American Adolescents," https://www.mghstudentwellness.org/resources-1/guide-for-parents-of-asianasian-american-adolescents; Massachusetts General Hospital Student Wellness, "Talking to Teens About Anti-Asian Discrimination in the Era of Covid-19: Guidance from Research and Practice," March 5, 2021, https://vimeo.com/520018357.

104   Embrace Race, https://www.embracerace.org/; Public Broadcasting Service, "Talking to Young Children About Race and Racism," https://www.pbs.org/parents/talking-about-racism.

105   Charlene Wong, "Fancy Terminology," Judge-Me-Not: By My Circumstances (website), https://judge-me-not.weebly.com/fancy-terminology.html; Natalya Dell, "Intersecting Axes of Privilege, Domination, and Oppression," Natalyad (website), February 10, 2014, https://sites.google.com/site/natalyadell/home/intersectionality; Kathryn Pauly Morgan et al., "Describing the Emperor's New Clothes: Three Myths of Educational (In-)Equality, The Gender Question in Education," *Theory, Pedagogy and Politics* 105, no. 1 (1996).

106   John Cho, "Coronavirus Reminds Asian Americans Like Me That Our Belonging is Conditional," *Los Angeles Times,* April 22, 2020, https://www.latimes.com/opinion/story/2020-04-22/asian-american-discrimination-john-cho-coronavirus.

107   Audiey Kao, "Interview with Jennifer Ho," University of Colorado, Boulder, June 2020, https://journalofethics.ama-assn.org/videocast/ethics-talk-spread-anti-asian-racism-and-xenophobia-during-covid-19-pandemic.

108   Kelsey Simpkins, "Anti-Asian Discrimination Amid Pandemic Spurs Jennifer Ho to Action," *CU Boulder Today,* April 17, 2020, https://www.colorado.edu/today/2020/04/17/anti-asian-discrimination-amid-pandemic-spurs-jennifer-ho-action.

109   Association of Asian American Studies, "AAAS Statement on Anti-Asian Harassment and the Novel Coronavirus/Covid-19," March 5, 2020, https://aaastudies.org/aaas-statement-on-anti-asian-harassment-and-the-novel-coronavirus-covid-19/.

110   Jennifer Ho, "Anti-Asian Racism and Covid-19," *Colorado Arts and Science Magazine,* revised July 16, 2020, https://www.colorado.edu/asmagazine/2020/04/08/anti-asian-racism-and-covid-19.

111 Dismantling Racism, *Racism Defined,* https://www. dismantlingracism.org/racism-defined.html.

112 Dismantling Racism.

113 Claudio Saunt, "The Invasion of America," *Aeon,* January 7, 2015, https://aeon.co/essays/how-were-1-5-billion-acres-of-land-so-rapidly-stolen.

114 Slave Voyages, website, https://www.slavevoyages.org/.

115 Densho, "Preserving Japanese American Stories of the Past for the Generations of Tomorrow," website, https://densho.org.

116 Adam Serwer, "A Crime by Any Name," *The Atlantic,* July 3, 2019, https://www.theatlantic.com/ideas/archive/2019/07/border-facilities/593239/.

117 Bruce Mitchell and Juan Franco, "HOLC 'Redlining' Maps: The Persistent Structure of Segregation and Economic Inequality," National Community Reinvestment Coalition, March 20, 2018, https://ncrc.org/holc/.

118 Marisa Peñaloza, "'Illicit Cohabitation': Listen To 6 Stunning Moments from Loving v. Virginia," NPR, June 12, 2017, https://www.npr.org/2017/06/12/532123349/illicit-cohabitation-listen-to-6-stunning-moments-from-loving-v-virginia.

119 United States Courts, "History—Brown v. Board of Education Re-Enactment," https://www.uscourts.gov/educational-resources/educational-activities/history-brown-v-board-education-re-enactment.

120 Timothy D. Wilson and Daniel T. Gilbert, "Explaining Away: A Model of Affective Adaptation," *Perspectives on Psychological Science* 3, (2008): 370.

121 Marc Ramirez, "Who Gets to Decide What Is Racism, Hate? Atlanta Shootings Renew Debate over White Violence, Privilege," *USA Today,* March 18, 2021, https://www.usatoday.com/story/news/2021/03/18/atlanta-victims-were-killed-white-violence-racism-many-insist/4751240001/.

122 Nicole Hong and Jonah E. Bromwich, "Asian-Americans Are Being Attacked. Why Are Hate Crime Charges So Rare?" *The New York Times,* October 26, 2021, https://www.nytimes.com/2021/03/18/nyregion/asian-hate-crimes.html.

123   Angie Chuang, "Two Stereotypes that Diminish the Humanity of the Atlanta Shooting Victims—and All Asian Americans," *The Conversation,* March 26, 2021, https://theconversation.com/two-stereotypes-that-diminish-the-humanity-of-the-atlanta-shooting-victims-and-all-asian-americans-157762.

124   Meghan Roos, "Sheriff's Comments That Atlanta Shooter Had 'Really Bad Day' Sparks Backlash," *Newsweek,* March 17, 2021, https://www.newsweek.com/sheriffs-comments-that-atlanta-shooter-had-really-bad-day-sparks-backlash-1576936.

125   Stephanie K. Baer, "The Cop Who Said the Spa Shooter Had a 'Bad Day' Previously Posted a Racist Shirt Blaming China for the Pandemic," *BuzzFeed News,* March 17, 2021, https://www.buzzfeednews.com/article/skbaer/spa-shooter-bad-day-racist-facebook (showing the Facebook post photo).

126   Nancy Guan, "'We Need Protection': Georgia State Sen. Michelle Au Warned of Anti-Asian Violence Before Atlanta Shootings," *USA Today,* March 20, 2021, https://www.usatoday.com/story/news/nation/2021/03/20/atlanta-shooting-state-sen-michelle-au-condemns-anti-asian-violence/4781935001/.

127   Editorial Board, "Asian-Americans Are Scared for a Reason," *The New York Times,* March 18, 2021, https://www.nytimes.com/2021/03/18/opinion/anti-asian-american-violence.html.

128   Kara Swisher, "An Asian American Poet on Refusing to Take Up 'Apologetic Space,'" *The New York Times,* April 1, 2021, https://www.nytimes.com/2021/04/01/opinion/sway-kara-swisher-cathy-park-hong.html.

129   Marc Ramirez, "Stop Asian Hate, Stop Black Hate, Stop All Hate: Many Americans Call for Unity Against Racism," *USA Today,* March 22, 2021, https://www.usatoday.com/story/news/nation/2021/03/20/atlanta-shootings-see-asian-black-americans-take-white-supremacy/4769268001/.

130   Marc Ramirez and Trevor Hughes, "'Stand Up, Fight Back': Atlanta Rally Decries Anti-Asian Violence, Mourns Spa Shooting Victims," *USA Today,* March 21, 2021, https://www.usatoday.com/story/news/nation/2021/03/20/atlanta-shooting-surveillance-video-aaron-long-march-victims/4780302001/.

131   Brian X. Chen, "There Is No Rung on the Ladder That Protects You from Hate," *The New York Times*, March 24, 2021, https://www.nytimes.com/2021/03/20/technology/personaltech/asian-american-wealth-gap.html.

132   Marc Ramirez, "Asian American Activists Are Demanding Equal Civil Rights, Better Education in Schools After Asian Hate Attacks," *USA Today*, March 27, 2021, https://www.usatoday.com/story/news/nation/2021/03/26/stop-asian-hate-asian-americans-across-us-demand-reforms/6990150002/.

133   House Committee on the Judiciary, "Discrimination and Violence Against Asian Americans," YouTube, March 18, 2021, https://youtu.be/547JYf-VA_Q.

134   Catie Edmondson, "Asian-American Lawmakers Call Out Racist Language: 'I Am Not a Virus,'" *The New York Times*, May 5, 2021, https://www.nytimes.com/2021/03/18/us/politics/asian-politicians-racism.html.

135   Catie Edmondson, "House Democrats Hold a Rare Congressional Hearing on Anti-Asian Discrimination," *The New York Times*, March 18, 2021, https://www.nytimes.com/2021/03/18/us/congress-hearing-asian-american-discrimination.html.

136   House Committee on the Judiciary.

137   House Committee on the Judiciary. See also Federal Bureau of Investigation, "2019 Hate Crime Statistics," Uniform Crime Reporting Program, https://ucr.fbi.gov/hate-crime/2019/topic-pages/incidents-and-offenses.

138   House Committee on the Judiciary. See also US Bureau of Labor Statistics, "Asian Women and Men Earned More Than Their White, Black, and Hispanic Counterparts in 2017," August 29, 2018, https://www.bls.gov/opub/ted/2018/asian-women-and-men-earned-more-than-their-white-black-and-hispanic-counterparts-in-2017.htm.

139   House Committee on the Judiciary.

140   Michael D. Shear, "Confronting Violence Against Asians, Biden Says That 'We Cannot Be Complicit,'" *The New York Times*, March 19, 2021, https://www.nytimes.com/2021/03/19/us/politics/biden-harris-atlanta.html.

141   S. 937, 117th Congress, (2021); H.R. 6721, 116th Cong. (2020).

142 S. 2043, 116th Congress, (2019).

143 National Defense Authorization Act for Fiscal Year 2010, Pub. L. No. 111-84, 123 Stat. 2190.

144 Larissa Lam and Baldwin Chiu, *Far East Deep South,* documentary film, 2020, https://fareastdeepsouth.com/.

145 Roseann Liu, "Dismantling the Barrier Between Asians and African Americans," *The Philadelphia Inquirer,* June 8, 2018, https://www.inquirer.com/philly/opinion/stop-and-go-asian-african-americans-20180608.html.

146 John Jung, *Chopsticks in the Land of Cotton: Lives of Mississippi Delta Chinese Grocers,* (Yin and Yang Press, 2008), p. 89, 108.

147 Kenneth J. Arrow, *Racial Discrimination in Economic Life,* 187; Kenneth J. Arrow, *Discrimination in Labor Markets,* 3; Edmund S. Phelps, "The Statistical Theory of Racism and Sexism," *American Economic Review* 62 (1972): 659; Michael Spence, "Job Market Signaling," *Quarterly Journal of Economics* 87, (1973): 355, 368–374; Joseph E. Stiglitz, "Approaches to the Economics of Discrimination," *American Economic Review* 63, (1973): 287.

148 Mike Moffat, "The Economics of Discrimination: An Examination of the Economic Theory of Statistical Discrimination," ThoughtCo., April 10, 2019, https://www.thoughtco.com/the-economics-of-discrimination-1147202.

149 Isheka N. Harrison, "7 Things to Know About Howard University Economist William Spriggs," Moguldom Nation, October 12, 2020, https://moguldom.com/310025/7-things-to-know-about-howard-university-economist-william-spriggs/.

150 William Spriggs, "A Teachable Moment? Will George Floyd's Death Spur Change in Economics?" Federal Reserve Bank of Minneapolis, June 9, 2020, https://www.minneapolisfed.org/article/2020/a-teachable-moment-will-george-floyds-death-spur-change-in-economics.

151 Nadra Kareem Nittle, "What Is a Stereotype?" ThoughtCo., February 4, 2021, https://www.thoughtco.com/what-is-the-meaning-of-stereotype-2834956.

152 Njeri Mathis Rutledge, South Texas College of Law Houston, http://www.stcl.edu/about-us/faculty/njeri-i-mathis-rutledge/; Njeri Mathis Rutledge, Curriculum Vitae, http://www.stcl.edu/wp-content/uploads/2016/08/Rutledge.cv_.2016.pdf.

153 Njeri Rutledge, "I Thought I Never Personally Experienced Racism. Then I Realized I Just Normalized It," *USA Today*, September 15, 2020, https://www.usatoday.com/story/opinion/voices/2020/09/15/racism-every-day-black-women-column/5793258002/.

154 Rutledge.

155 Damon Young, "The Definition, Danger and Disease of Respectability Politics, Explained," *The Root,* March 21, 2016, https://www.theroot.com/the-definition-danger-and-disease-of-respectdability-po-1790854699.

156 Sarah Molano, "The Problem with Respectability Politics, Pipe Dream," April 23, 2018, https://www.bupipedream.com/opinions/94369/the-problem-with-respectability-politics/.

157 Tracy Jan, "Asian American Doctors and Nurses Are Fighting Racism and the Coronavirus," *The Washington Post*, May 19, 2020, https://www.washingtonpost.com/business/2020/05/19/asian-american-discrimination/.

158 Andrew Yang, "Andrew Yang: We Asian Americans Are Not the Virus, but We Can Be Part of the Cure," *The Washington Post,* April 1, 2020, https://www.washingtonpost.com/opinions/2020/04/01/andrew-yang-coronavirus-discrimination/.

159 George Takei, Twitter, April 7, 2020, https://twitter.com/GeorgeTakei/status/1246139544115777542.

160 Steven Yeun, Twitter, April 3, 2020, https://twitter.com/steveyeun/status/1246186737455357952.

161 Simu Liu, Twitter, April 2, 2020, https://twitter.com/SimuLiu/status/1245886734337859584.

162 Jenn Fang, "Andrew Yang Is Wrong: Respectability Politics Won't Save Asian Americans from Racist Violence," *Reappropriate,* April 2, 2020, http://reappropriate.co/2020/04/andrew-yang-is-wrong-respectability-politics-wont-save-asian-americans-from-racist-violence/.

163   Dismantling Racism.

164   Ad Council, "Fight the Virus. Fight the Bias. Love Has No Labels,"
       YouTube, July 21, 2020, https://youtu.be/5ocfEGYD_Xw.

165   Tiffany Hsu, "Anti-Asian Harassment Is Surging. Can Ads and
       Hashtags Help?" *The New York Times*, July 21, 2020, https://
       www.nytimes.com/2020/07/21/business/media/asian-american-
       harassment-ad-council.html.

166   Tiffany Hsu, "A New P.S.A. Hopes to Put a Focus on Pandemic-
       Related Racism," *The New York Times*, July 21, 2020, https://www.
       nytimes.com/2020/07/21/business/a-new-psa-hopes-to-put-a-focus-
       on-pandemic-related-racism.html.

167   National Committee on U.S.-China Relations, "The 'Model
       Minority' Myth: Jennifer Ho and Frank H. Wu," YouTube, August 6,
       2020, https://youtu.be/zHFvEvPo5z0.

168   Albert O. Hirschman, *Exit, Voice and Loyalty: Responses to
       Decline in Firms, Organizations, and States,* (Cambridge: Harvard
       University Press, 1970).

169   National Committee on U.S.-China Relations.

170   Alisha Haridasani Gupta, "A Teacher Held a Famous Racism
       Exercise in 1968. She's Still at It," *The New York Times*, July 15,
       2020, https://www.nytimes.com/2020/07/04/us/jane-elliott-anti-
       racism-blue-eyes-brown-eyes.html.

171   Jane Elliott, *A Collar in My Pocket: Blue Eyes/Brown Eyes Exercise*,
       (Self-Published, 2016).

172   Public Broadcasting Service, "A Class Divided," *Frontline,* YouTube,
       January 18, 2019, https://youtu.be/1mcCLm_LwpE.

173   Jimmy Fallon, "Jane Elliott on Her 'Blue Eyes/Brown Eyes
       Exercise' and Fighting Racism," *The Tonight Show*, YouTube, June
       2, 2020, https://youtu.be/f2z-ahJ4uws.

174   Sam McFarland, "Identification with All Humanity: The
       Antithesis of Prejudice, and More," in *Cambridge Handbook of the
       Psychology of Prejudice,* (Cambridge University Press, 2018), pp.
       632, 652–54.

175   Brianna Holt, "The Return of Jane Elliott," *The New York Times*, July 24, 2020, https://www.nytimes.com/2020/07/15/style/jane-elliott-anti-racism.html.

176   Nathan Rutstein, *Healing Racism in America: A Prescription for the Disease*, (Star Commonwealth, 1993), p. 99.

177   Daniel McGann-Bartleman, "If You're a Bystander, You're a Racist," *The Breeze*, October 13, 2016, https://www.breezejmu.org/opinion/if-youre-a-bystander-youre-a-racist/article_d7d83444-90cc-11e6-870c-4b9e8554a534.html.

178   Tracy Jan, "As They Fight Virus, Asian Americans Battle Racism," *The Washington Post*, May 22, 2020.

179   George A. Akerlof and Rachel E. Kranton, "Economics and Identity," *Quarterly Journal of Economics* 115, (2000): 715.

180   Claire A. Hill, "The Law and Economics of Identity," *Queen's Law Journal* 32, (2007): 389.

181   Robyn A. LeBoeuf et al., "The Conflicting Choices of Alternating Selves," *Organizational Behavior and Human Decision Processes* 111, (2010): 48, 52.

182   Eduardo Bonilla-Silva, "Feeling Race: Theorizing the Racial Economy of Emotions," *American Sociological Review* 84, (2019): 1-2.

183   Martin Luther King Jr., "The Other America," speech delivered on April 14, 1967, transcript available at https://www.crmvet.org/docs/otheram.htm.

184   Jenny Yang, Twitter, April 3, 2020, https://twitter.com/jennyyangtv/status/1246132396191178752.

185   Jenny Yang.

186   Rebecca Sun, "Comedian Jenny Yang Rebuts Andrew Yang Op-Ed with Satirical Video: 'Honk If You Won't Hate-Crime Me!'" *Hollywood Reporter*, April 5, 2020, https://www.hollywoodreporter.com/news/comedian-jenny-yang-rebuts-andrew-yang-op-ed-satirical-video-1288623.

187   Benny Luo, "Andrew Yang Responds to Backlash on *The Washington Post* Op-Ed," Nextshark, April 7, 2020, https://nextshark.com/andrew-yang-responds-washington-post-op-ed/.

188   Gordon W. Allport, *The Nature of Prejudice*, (Basic Books, 1979).

189   Thomas E. Ford et al., "More Than 'Just a Joke': The Prejudice-
       Releasing Function of Sexist Humor," *Personality and Social
       Psychology Bulletin* 34, (2008): 159; Nicholas Kristof, "To Beat
       Trump, Mock Him," *The New York Times*, September 26, 2020,
       https://www.nytimes.com/2020/09/26/opinion/sunday/trump-
       politics-humor.html; Robyn K. Mallett et al., "What Did He
       Mean By That? Humor Decreases Attributions of Sexism and
       Confrontation of Sexist Jokes," *Sex Roles* 75, (2016): 272.

190   Jennifer Aaker and Naomi Bagdonas, *Humor, Seriously: Why
       Humor Is a Secret Weapon in Business and Life (And How Anyone
       Can Harness It. Even You),* (Currency Press: 2021), p. 15.

191   Dana Bilsky Asher, "The Surprising Link Between Laughter and
       Learning," *Fast Company,* May 10, 2016, https://www.fastcompany.
       com/3059651/the-surprising-link-between-laughter-and-learning;
       see also Avner Ziv, "Teaching and Learning with Humor:
       Experiment and Replication," *Journal of Experimental Education*
       57, (1988): 5.

192   Colette Hoption et al., "It's Not You, It's Me: Transformational
       Leadership and Self-Deprecating Humor," *Leadership and
       Organizational Development Journal* 34, (2013): 4; see also Nale
       Lehmann-Willenbrock and Joseph A. Allen, "How Fun Are Your
       Meetings? Investigating the Relationship Between Humor
       Patterns in Team Interactions and Team Performance," *Journal of
       Applied Psychology* 99, (2014): 1278.

193   Tali Sharot and Cass R. Sunstein, "How People Decide What They
       Want to Know," *Nature Human Behavior* 4, (2020): 14.

194   NBC, "White Like Me," *Saturday Night Live,* December 15, 1984,
       https://www.nbc.com/saturday-night-live/video/white-like-me/
       n9308 [https://perma.cc/VTF7-WBQD].

195   John Howard Griffin, *Black Like Me*, (Berkley, 2010).

196   Todd B. Kashdan, "The Science Behind Holding Your Identity(s)
       Loosely," The Growth Equation (website), https://thegrowtheq.
       com/the-science-behind-holding-your-identitys-loosely/.

197   Patricia W. Linville, "Self-Complexity As a Cognitive Buffer Against
       Stress-Related Illness and Depression," *Journal of Personality and
       Social Psychology* 52, (1987): 663–667.

198   Patricia W. Linville, "Self-Complexity and Affective Extremity: Don't Put All of Your Eggs in One Cognitive Basket," *Social Cognition* 3, (1985): 94-120.

199   Deborah Cantrell, "Exploring Transformative Silence and Protest," *Rutgers Journal of Law and Religion* 22, (2021): 83.

200   *The Late Show with Stephen Colbert,* "Keegan-Michael Key: My Encounters with Police Are Different As a Famous Black Man," YouTube, June 3, 2020, https://youtu.be/2A6I_a3EJwc.

201   Chimamanda Ngozi Adichie, "The Danger of a Single Story," TEDGlobal, 2009, https://www.ted.com/talks/chimamanda_ngozi_adichie_the_danger_of_a_single_story.

202   Procter & Gamble, "Widen the Screen to Widen Our View," https://us.pg.com/widen-the-screen/.

203   See web.pdx.edu/~tothm/pluralism/street calculus.pdf.

204   Michele Norris, "Six Words: 'You've Got To Be Taught' Intolerance," NPR, *Morning Edition,* May 19, 2014, https://www.npr.org/2014/05/19/308296815/six-words-youve-got-to-be-taught-intolerance.

205   Richard Rodgers and Oscar Hammerstein II, "You've Got to be Carefully Taught," *South Pacific,* YouTube, August 3, 2018, https://www.youtube.com/watch?v=VPf6ITsjsgk.

206   Andrea Most, "'You've Got to be Carefully Taught': The Politics of Race in Rodgers and Hammerstein's *South Pacific,*" *Theatre Journal* 52, (2000): 307.

207   Robert P. Abelson, "Beliefs Are Like Possessions," *Journal for the Theory of Social Behaviour* 16, (1984): 223.

208   George Loewenstein, *Exotic Preferences: Behavioral Economics and Human Motivation,* (Oxford University Press, 2008).

209   "Clinton on Implicit Bias in Policing," *The Washington Post,* September 26, 2016, https://www.washingtonpost.com/video/politics/clinton-on-implicit-bias-in-policing/2016/09/26/46e1e88c-8441-11e6-b57d-dd49277af02f_video.html.

210   Dan Merica, "Hillary Clinton Talks Race: 'We All Have Implicit Biases,'" CNN, April 20, 2016, https://www.cnn.com/2016/04/20/politics/hillary-clinton-race-implicit-biases/index.html.

211 Anthony G. Greenwald and Linda Hamilton Krieger, "Implicit Bias: Scientific Foundations," *California Law Review* 94, (2006): 945, 955-956; Jerry Matysik, "Implicit Bias and Law Enforcement: Reducing Blame and Understanding the Brain," Lexipol, February 15, 2017, https://www.lexipol.com/resources/blog/implicit-bias-law-enforcement-reducing-blame-understanding-brain/.

212 Howard University School of Law, "Social Justice: Implicit Bias and Microaggressions," https://library.law.howard.edu/socialjustice/bias.

213 Charles M. Pierce, "Black Psychiatry One Year After Miami," *Journal of National Medical Association* 62, (1970): 471-472; see also Tori DeAngelis, "Unmasking 'Racial Microaggressions,'" *Monitor* 40, (2009): 42, https://www.apa.org/monitor/2009/02/microaggression.

214 Staff Writer, "What Is a Microaggression?" *Psychology Today,* https://www.psychologytoday.com/us/basics/microaggression.

215 Derald Wing Sue et al., "Racial Microaggressions in Everyday Life: Implications for Clinical Practice," *American Psychologist* 62, (2007): 271.

216 Derald Wing Sue and Lisa Spanierman, *Microaggressions in Everyday Life: Race, Gender, and Sexual Orientation,* (Wiley, 2010).

217 Scott O. Lilienfeld, "Microaggressions: Strong Claims, Inadequate Evidence," *Perspectives on Psychological Science* 12, (2017): 138.

218 Conor Friedersdorf, "Why Critics of the 'Microaggressions' Framework Are Skeptical," *The Atlantic,* September 4, 2015, https://www.theatlantic.com/politics/archive/2015/09/why-critics-of-the-microaggressions-framework-are-skeptical/405106/.

219 Edward Cantu and Lee Jussim, "Microaggressions, Questionable Science, and Free Speech," *Texas Review of Law and Politics* 26, (2021): 217.

220 Greg Lukianoff and Jonathan Haidt, *The Coddling of the American Mind: How Good Intentions and Bad Ideas Are Setting Up a Generation for Failure* (Penguin Press, 2018).

221 State v. Bridges 133 N.J. 447 (1993) 628 A.2d 270.

222   Tracey Tully, "Debate Erupts at N.J. Law School After White Student Quotes Racial Slur," *The New York Times*, May 3, 2021, https://www.nytimes.com/2021/05/03/nyregion/Rutgers-law-school-n-word.html; Eugene Volokh, "Rutgers Law Students Calling for a 'Policy' on Students and Faculty Quoting Slurs from Court Cases," Volokh Conspiracy, May 3, 2021, https://reason.com/volokh/2021/05/03/rutgers-law-students-calling-for-a-policy-on-students-and-faculty-quoting-slurs-from-court-cases/; Debra Cassens Weiss, "Law Student Who Quoted from Opinion, Including its Racial Slur, Finds Herself at Center of Controversy," *American Bar Association Journal,* May 4, 2021, https://www.abajournal.com/news/article/law-student-who-quoted-from-opinion-including-its-racial-slur-finds-herself-at-center-of-controversy.

223   Volokh Conspiracy.

224   Ginia Bellafante, "Private Schools Brought in Diversity Consultants. Outrage Ensued," *The New York Times*, April 23, 2021, https://www.nytimes.com/2021/04/23/nyregion/private-schools-diversity-brearley-dalton-grace.html.

225   University of Connecticut School of Law, "Implicit Bias in the Courts," https://libguides.law.uconn.edu/implicit/courts.

226   Michelle Silverthorn, "5 Ways Law Students Can Interrupt Implicit Bias, Diversity," Student Lawyer Blog, American Bar Association, May 29, 2018, https://abaforlawstudents.com/2018/05/29/5-ways-law-students-can-interrupt-implicit-bias/.

227   National Center for State Courts, "Implicit Bias," https://www.ncsc.org/information-and-resources/racial-justice/implicit-bias.

228   Shawn C. Marsh, "The Lens of Implicit Bias," National Center for Juvenile Justice, 2009, https://www.ncjfcj.org/publications/the-lens-of-implicit-bias/.

229   National Initiative for Building Community Trust and Justice, "Implicit Bias," https://trustandjustice.org/resources/intervention/implicit-bias.

230   Kathryn Stanchi, "The Rhetoric of Racism in the United States Supreme Court," *Boston College Law Review* 62, (2021): 1251.

231   Michael Selmi, "The Paradox of Implicit Bias and a Plea for a New Narrative," *Arizona State Law Journal* 50, (2018): 193.

232 Anne Warfield Rawls and Waverly Duck, *Tacit Racism,* (University of Chicago Press, 2020).

233 George Loewenstein and Andras Molnar, "The Renaissance of Belief-Based Utility in Economics," *Nature Human Behavior* 2, (2018): 166; Andras Molnar and George Loewenstein, "Thoughts and Players: An Introduction to Old and New Economic Perspectives on Beliefs," in *The Cognitive Science of Beliefs: A Multidisciplinary Approach,* ed. Julien Musolino, (Cambridge University Press, 2022), pp. 321-350.

234 Ronit Bodner and Drazen Prelec, "Self-Signaling and Diagnostic Utility in Everyday Decision Making," in *The Psychology of Economic Decisions, Volume 1: Rationality and Well-Being,* eds. Isabelle Brocas and Juab D. Carrillo, (Oxford University Press, 2003), p. 105.

235 Ralph Hertwig and Christoph Engel, eds., *Deliberate Ignorance: Choosing Not to Know,* (MIT Press, 2021).

236 Charles M. Blow, "Is America a Racist Country?" *The New York Times*, May 2, 2021, https://www.nytimes.com/2021/05/02/opinion/america-racism.html.

237 Ralph Richard Banks, "Beyond Colorblindness: Neo-Racialism and the Future of Race and Law Scholarship," *Harvard Blackletter Law Journal* 25, (2009): 41.

238 Serena Chow, "The Mental Health Implications of Covid-19 Related Violence Against Asian Americans," *Asian American News,* April 30, 2020, https://asamnews.com/2020/04/30/rise-in-anti-asian-hate-crimes-expected-to-adversely-impact-mental-health-of-asian-americans/; Ivan Natividad, "Racist Harassment of Asian Health Care Workers Won't Cure Coronavirus," *Berkeley News,* April 9, 2020, https://news.berkeley.edu/2020/04/09/racist-harassment-of-asian-health-care-workers-wont-cure-coronavirus/; Jenny T. Wang, *Permission to Come Home: Reclaiming Mental Health as Asian Americans,* (Balance, 2022).

239 Christopher L. Eisgruber, "Letter from President Eisgruber on the University's Efforts to Combat Systemic Racism," Princeton University, September 2, 2020, https://www.princeton.edu/news/2020/09/02/letter-president-eisgruber-universitys-efforts-combat-systemic-racism.

240   Sergiu Klainerman, "Princeton's President Is Wrong. The University Is Not Systemically Racist," *Newsweek,* September 9, 2020, https://www.newsweek.com/princetons-president-wrong-university-not-systemically-racist-opinion-1530480.

241   Paul Mirengoff, "Northwestern Law Dean Says He's A Racist," Power Line, November 1, 2020, https://www.powerlineblog.com/archives/2020/11/northwestern-law-dean-says-hes-a-racist.php.

242   Sandra E. Garcia, "Where Did BIPOC Come From?" *The New York Times*, June 17, 2020, https://www.nytimes.com/article/what-is-bipoc.html.

243   Andrew W. Lo and Ruixun Zhang, "The Wisdom of Crowds Versus the Madness of Mobs: An Evolutionary Model of Bias, Polarization, and Other Challenges to Collective Intelligence," *Collective Intelligence* 1, (2022): 1.

244   MIT Sloan School Office of Media Relations, "New Study Suggests Evolutionary Forces Are Behind Collective Discrimination," November 10, 2022, https://mitsloan.mit.edu/press/new-study-suggests-evolutionary-forces-are-behind-collective-discrimination.

245   Lo and Zhang, 16.

246   Kenneth J. Arrow, "I Know a Hawk from a Handsaw," in *Eminent Economists: Their Life Philosophies,* ed. Michael Szenberg, (Cambridge University Press, 1993), p. 46.

247   Arithmetic of Compassion, website, https://www.arithmeticofcompassion.org/.

248   Daniel Politi, "Donald Trump in Phoenix: Mexicans Are 'Taking Our Jobs' and 'Killing Us,'" *Slate,* July 12, 2015, https://slate.com/news-and-politics/2015/07/donald-trump-in-phoenix-mexicans-are-taking-our-jobs-and-killing-us.html.

249   Anne Frank House, "Hitler's Antisemitism. Why Did He Hate the Jews?" https://www.annefrank.org/en/anne-frank/go-in-depth/why-did-hitler-hate-jews/.

250   Jennifer Szalai, "'The Sum of Us' Tallies the Cost of Racism for Everyone," *The New York Times*, February 23, 2021, https://www.nytimes.com/2021/02/23/books/review-sum-of-us-heather-mcghee.html.

251   Szalai.

252   Ran Abramitzky and Leah Boustan, *Streets of Gold: America's Untold Story of Immigrant Success,* (PublicAffairs, 2022).

253   Warfare History Network, "Hitler's Biggest Mistake: Why The Nazi Atomic Bomb Never Happened," National Interest, October 16, 2020, https://nationalinterest.org/blog/buzz/hitlers-biggest-mistake-why-nazi-atomic-bomb-never-happened-170800/.

254   Andrew Robinson, "'I Shall Never Forget the Kindness.' How England Helped Albert Einstein Escape Nazi Germany," *Time,* October 1, 2019, https://time.com/5684504/einstein-england/.

255   Dan Charles, "Heisenberg's Principles Kept Bomb from Nazis," *New Scientist,* September 5, 1992, https://www.newscientist.com/article/mg13518370-300-heisenbergs-principles-kept-bomb-from-nazis/.

256   Michael Gibbs, "Job Design, Learning and Intrinsic Motivation," University of Chicago Booth School of Business, Working Paper No. 21-11, April 11, 2021, https://papers.ssrn.com/sol3/papers.cfm?abstract_id=3824874.

257   Andrew Bloomenthal, "Agency Costs," Investopedia, March 28, 2021, https://www.investopedia.com/terms/a/agencycosts.asp.

258   Bengt Holmstrom, "Moral Hazard in Teams," *The Bell Journal of Economics* 13, (1982): 324.

259   Paul Milgrom and John D. Roberts, "Bargaining Costs, Influence Costs, and the Organization of Economic Activity," in *The Economic Nature of the Firm: A Reader,* eds. Randall S. Kroszner and Louis Putterman, (Cambridge University Press, 2014).

260   Ariana Ayu, "The Enormous Cost of Unhappy Employees," *Inc.,* August 27, 2014, https://www.inc.com/ariana-ayu/the-enormous-cost-of-unhappy-employees.html.

261   Arline T. Geronimus et al., "Do US Black Women Experience Stress-Related Accelerated Biological Aging? A Novel Theory and First Population-Based Test of Black-White Differences in Telomere Length," *Human Nature* 21, (2010): 19.

262   Eve Ekman and Jeremy Adam Smith, "When Racism Makes Us Sick," in *Are We Born Racist? New Insights from Neuroscience and Positive Psychology*, eds. Jason Marsh et al., (Beacon Press, 2010), p. 34.

263   Elizabeth Page-Gould, "The Unhealthy Racist," in *Are We Born Racist? New Insights from Neuroscience and Positive Psychology*, eds. Jason Marsh et al., (Beacon Press, 2010), p. 41.

264   Page-Gould, "The Unhealthy Racist," 41.

265   Page-Gould, "The Unhealthy Racist," 42.

266   Page-Gould, "The Unhealthy Racist," 42.

267   Wendy Berry Mendes et al., "Why Egalitarianism Might Be Good for Your Health: Physiological Thriving During Stressful Intergroup Encounters," *Psychological Science* 18, (2007): 991.

268   Elizabeth Page-Gould et al., "With A Little Help from My Cross-Group Friend: Reducing Anxiety in Intergroup Contexts through Cross-Group Friendships," *Journal of Personality and Social Psychology* 95, (2008): 1080.

269   Jim Blascovich et al., "Perceiver Threat in Social Interactions with Stigmatized Others," *Journal of Personality and Social Psychology* 80, (2001): 253.

270   Page-Gould, "The Unhealthy Racist," 42-43.

271   Page-Gould, "The Unhealthy Racist," 44.

272   Leonard J. Savage, *The Foundations of Statistics,* (Dover Publications, 1972); see also Leonard J. Savage, "Theory of Statistical Decision," *Journal of the American Statistical Association* 46, (1951): 55.

273   John W. Pratt, Howard Raiffa, and Robert Schlaifer, *Introduction to Statistical Decision Theory*, (MIT Press, 2008).

274   Grundfest and Huang.

275   Pierpaolo Battigalli and Martin Dufwenberg, "Belief-Dependent Motivations and Psychological Game Theory," *Journal of Economic Literature* 60, (2022): 833-882; John Geanakoplos et al., "Psychological Games and Sequential Rationality," *Games and Economic Behavior* 1, (1989): 60; see also Ofer H. Azar, "The Influence of Psychological Game Theory," *Games and Economic Behavior* 167, (2019): 459.

276   Peter H. Huang and Ho-Mou Wu, "Emotional Responses in Litigation," *International Review of Law and Economics* 12, (1992): 31.

277   Peter H. Huang and Ho-Mou Wu, "More Order Without More Law: A Theory of Social Norms and Organizational Cultures," *Journal of Law, Economics, and Organization* 10, (1992): 390, 394.

278   Peter H. Huang, "Pandemic Emotions: The Good, the Bad, and the Unconscious—Implications for Public Health, Financial Economics, Law, and Leadership," *Northwestern Journal of Law and Social Policy* 16, (2021): 80, 127-29.

279   Thomas C. Schelling, "The Mind as a Consuming Organ," in *The Multiple Self,* ed. Jon Elster, (Cambridge University Press, 1987), pp. 177, 180.

280   Schelling, 183.

281   Schelling, 193.

282   Schelling, 184-195.

283   Andras Molnar, personal website, https://www.amolnar.com/.

284   Molnar.

285   Hertwig et al., *Deliberate Ignorance.*

286   Hertwig et al., *Deliberate Ignorance.*

287   Robert Wright, *The Moral Animal: Why We Are the Way We Are: The New Science of Evolutionary Psychology,* (Vintage Press, 1995), p. 280.

288   Peter H. Huang, "Book Review of *Why the Law Is So Perverse,*" *Journal of Legal Education* 63, (2013): 131, 138-48, https://jle.aals.org/home/vol63/iss1/9/.

289   Eyal Zamir and Roi Yair, in *Deliberate Ignorance,* p. 299.

290   Lonnie G. Bunch III, "We are American, and We Stand Together: Asian American Resilience, Belonging and Justice," remarks at the Smithsonian Asian Pacific American Center, May 15, 2021, YouTube, https://youtu.be/Lm0T-EQluiU.

291   Kenneth J. Arrow, in *Creating a Learning Society: A New Approach to Growth, Development, and Social Progress,* by Joseph E. Stiglitz and Bruce C. Greenwald, (Columbia University Press, 2014), p. 507.

292   Bunch III, "Asian American Resilience."

293   Elizabeth M. Wheaton, *The Economics of Human Rights,* (Routledge, 2018).

294   Wheaton, back cover.

295   Wheaton, 256.

296   Wheaton, 256, 289.

297   Semir Zeki and John Paul Romaya, "Neural Correlates of Hate," *PLOS One* 3, (2008): e3556.

298   Wheaton, 272-274.

299   Samuel Cameron, *The Economics of Hate,* (Edward Elgar Publishing, 2009); Samuel Cameron, "Widening the Economic Approach to Hatred," *Forum for Social Economics* 39, (2009): 19.

300   George A. Akerlof and Janet L. Yellen, "The Fair Wage Effort Hypothesis and Unemployment," *Quarterly Journal of Economics* 105, (1990): 255; Vai-Lam Mui, "The Economics of Envy," *Journal of Economic Behavior and Organization* 26, (1995): 311; Redzo Mujic and Andrew J. Oswald, "Is Envy Harmful to a Society's Psychological Health and Wellbeing? Longitudinal Study of 18,000 Adults," *Social Science and Medicine* 198, (2018): 103; Hal Varian, "Equity, Envy, and Efficiency," *Journal of Economic Theory* 9, (1974): 63.

301   Gary Becker, *A Treatise on the Family,* (Harvard University Press, 1993).

302   Lewis R. Gale et al., "An Economic Analysis of Hate Crime," *Eastern Economic Journal* 28, (2002): 203.

303   Edward L. Glaeser, "The Political Economy of Hatred," *Quarterly Journal of Economics* 120, (2005): 45.

304   Glaeser, 45.

305   United States Department of Justice, Civil Rights Division, "Learn More About Hate Crimes," https://www.justice.gov/hatecrimes/learn-about-hate-crimes/chart.

306   Federal Bureau of Investigation, "Hate Crimes," https://www.fbi.gov/investigate/civil-rights/hate-crimes.

307   David Brax, "Motives, Reasons, and Responsibility in Hate/Bias Crime Legislation," *Criminal Justice Ethics* 35, (2016): 230.

308   Brax, 230.

309   United States Department of Justice, Bureau of Justice Assistance, "A Policymakers' Guide to Hate Crimes," (March 1997), x, 20, 22.

310   United States Department of Justice, Civil Rights Division, "Hate Crime Laws," https://www.justice.gov/crt/hate-crime-laws.

311   18 U.S.C. § 249 (2009).

312   S.937 - Covid-19 Hate Crimes Act, 117th Congress (2021-2022).

313   Catie Edmondson, "Senate Resoundingly Passes Bill to Target Anti-Asian Hate Crimes," *The New York Times*, April 22, 2021, https://www.nytimes.com/2021/04/22/us/politics/senate-anti-asian-hate-crimes.html.

314   Catie Edmondson and Jim Tankersley, "Biden Is Set to Sign a Bill Addressing Hate Crimes Against Asian-Americans," *The New York Times*, May 20, 2021, https://www.nytimes.com/2021/05/20/us/politics/biden-asian-hate-crimes.html.

315   Edmondson, "Biden Set to Sign a Bill."

316   United States Department of Justice, Civil Rights Division, "Laws and Policies," https://www.justice.gov/hatecrimes/laws-and-policies.

317   US Department of Justice, "Laws and Policies."

318   US Department of Justice, "Laws and Policies." The states with hate crime laws and which do not require the collection of hate crimes data are Alabama, Alaska, Colorado, Delaware, Kansas, Mississippi, Missouri, Montana, New Hampshire, North Carolina, North Dakota, Ohio, South Dakota, Tennessee, Vermont, West Virginia, and Wisconsin. Among United States territories, Puerto Rico has hate crime laws and does not require the collection of hate crimes data, while the American Samoa, Guam, Northern

Mariana Islands, and the United States Virgin Islands have neither hate crime laws nor require the collection of hate crimes data.

319   United States Department of Justice, Civil Rights Division, State Specific Information, https://www.justice.gov/hatecrimes/state-specific-information.

320   Wisconsin v. Mitchell, 508 U.S. 476, 479 (1993).

321   Wisconsin v. Mitchell.

322   Thomas D. Brooks, "First Amendment Penalty Enhancement for Hate Crimes: Content Regulation, Questionable State Interests and Non-Traditional Sentencing," *Journal of Criminal Law and Criminology* 84, (1994): 703.

323   Chaplinsky v. New Hampshire, 315 U.S. 568, 572 (1942).

324   Leonard Wayne Summer, "Hate Crimes, Literature, and Speech," in *A Companion to Applied Ethics*, eds. R. G. Frey and Christopher Heath Wellman, (Wiley-Blackwell, 2005), p. 142.

325   United States Department of Justice, "Laws and Policies."

326   Ralph Richard Banks et al., *Racial Justice and Law: Cases and Materials,* (Foundation Press, 2016), pp. 730-759; Claire Hansen, "What is a Hate Crime?" *U.S. News and World Report,* April 27, 2021, https://www.usnews.com/news/national-news/articles/what-is-a-hate-crime.

327   Dan M. Kahan, "Two Liberal Fallacies in the Hate Crimes Debate," *Law and Philosophy* 20, (2001): 175, 183-185.

328   Kahan, 183-185.

329   Heidi M. Hurd and Michael S. Moore, "Punishing Hatred and Prejudice," *Stanford Law Review* 56, (2004).

330   Heidi M. Hurd, "Why Liberals Should Hate 'Hate Crime Legislation,'" *Law and Philosophy* 20, (2001): 215.

331   Nicole Hong and Jonah E. Bromwich, "Asian-Americans Are Being Attacked. Why Are Hate Crime Charges So Rare?" *The New York Times*, May 5, 2021, https://www.nytimes.com/2021/03/18/nyregion/asian-hate-crimes.html.

332   Jamison Chung et al., "Combating AAPI Hate," *The Regulatory Review,* May 8, 2021, https://www.theregreview.org/2021/05/08/saturday-seminar-combating-aapi-hate/.

333   Richard Fausset and Neil Vigdor, "8 People Killed in Atlanta-Area Massage Parlor Shootings," *The New York Times*, March 16, 2021, https://www.nytimes.com/2021/03/16/us/atlanta-shootings-massage-parlor.html.

334   Anna North, "Claims of 'Sex Addiction' Are a Distraction in the Atlanta Killings," *Vox,* March 18, 2021, https://www.vox.com/22336271/atlanta-shooter-sex-addiction-robert-aaron-long.

335   Regina Kim, "Atlanta Spa Shootings."

336   Nicholas Bogel-Burroughs, "Atlanta Spa Shootings Were Hate Crimes, Prosecutor Says," *The New York Times*, May 11, 2021, https://www.nytimes.com/2021/05/11/us/atlanta-spa-shootings-hate-crimes.html.

337   Hannah Knowles and Haisten Willis, "Prosecutor to Seek Hate-Crime Charges Against White Man Accused in Atlanta-Area Spa Killings," *The Washington Post*, May 11, 2021.

338   Knowles.

339   Daniel Victor, "Georgia Added a Hate-Crimes Law Last Year After the Death of Ahmaud Arbery," *The New York Times*, March 18, 2021, https://www.nytimes.com/2021/03/18/us/georgia-hate-crime-law.html.

340   Editorial Staff, "Ahmaud Arbery Shooting: A Timeline of the Case," *The New York Times*, April 19, 2021, https://www.nytimes.com/article/ahmaud-arbery-timeline.html.

341   OCGA § 17-10-1 (2000).

342   Associated Press, "Georgia Court Throws Out Hate Crimes Law," *NBC News,* Oct. 25, 2004, https://www.nbcnews.com/id/wbna6331341.

343   Botts v. State, 604 S.E.2d 512, 514 (2004).

344   Peter H. Huang, "Emotional Reactions to Law and Economics, Market Metaphors, and Rationality Rhetoric," in *Theoretical Foundations of Law and Economics*, ed. Mark D. White, (Cambridge University Press, 2008), p. 167; Peter H. Huang, "Dangers of

Monetary Commensurability: A Psychological Game Model of
Contagion," *University of Pennsylvania Law Review* 146, (1998):
1701.

345   William J. Baumol et al., *Contestable Markets and the Theory
of Industry Structure,* (Harcourt College Press, 1982); see also
William A. Brock, "Contestable Markets and the Theory of
Industry Structure: A Review Article," *Journal of Political Economy*
91, (1983): 1055.

346   Robert J. Shiller, "Narrative Economics," *American Economic
Review* 107, (2017): 967; see also Robert J. Shiller, *Narrative
Economics: How Stories Go Viral and Drive Major Economic Events,*
(Princeton University Press, 2019).

347   Sheelah Kolhatkar, "Robinhood's Big Gamble," *The New Yorker,*
May 17, 2021, https://www.newyorker.com/magazine/2021/05/17/
robinhoods-big-gamble.

348   John P. Anderson et al., "Social Media, Securities Markets, and the
Phenomenon of Expressive Trading," *Lewis and Clark Law Review*
25, (2022): 1223.

349   Susan Fader, "Narrative Economics: Reframing the Roles of
Storytelling and Behavioral Economics," *Qualitative Research
Consultants Association Views,* July 16, 2020, pp. 24-25, https://
qrcaviews.org/2020/07/16/narrative-economics-reframing-the-
roles-of-storytelling-and-behavioral-economics/.

350   Jon-Patrick Allem, "Social Media Fuels Wave of Coronavirus
Misinformation as Users Focus on Popularity, Not Accuracy," *The
Conversation,* April 6, 2020, https://theconversation.com/social-
media-fuels-wave-of-coronavirus-misinformation-as-users-focus-on-
popularity-not-accuracy-135179.

351   This might appear to be inconsistent with the discussion above
about how racism is bad for people. This tension is resolved in the
way that drinking or eating Twinkies (or doing both at once) is
bad for someone who nonetheless enjoys doing so.

352   Elizabeth Levy Paluck et al., "Prejudice Reduction: Progress and
Challenges," *Annual Review of Psychology* 72, (2021): 533.

353   Alia Wong, "Why Schools Are Banning Yoga," *The Atlantic,*
September 20, 2018, https://www.theatlantic.com/education/
archive/2018/09/why-schools-are-banning-yoga/570904/.

354   Martin E. P. Seligman et al., "Positive Education: Positive Psychology and Classroom Interventions," *Oxford Review of Education* 35, (2009): 293.

355   Natalie Allison, "Tennessee Republicans Want to Block Lessons on Systemic Racism in Schools," *USA Today*, May 3, 2021, https://www.usatoday.com/story/news/nation/2021/05/03/tennessee-republicans-take-critical-race-theory-lessons/4921671001/.

356   Emma Pettit, "The Academic Concept Conservative Lawmakers Love to Hate," *Chronicle of Higher Education,* May 12, 2020, https://www.chronicle.com/article/the-academic-concept-conservative-lawmakers-love-to-hate; Alia Wong, "Teaching Kids to Hate America? Republicans Want 'Critical Race Theory' Out of Schools," *USA Today*, May 13, 2021, https://www.usatoday.com/story/news/education/2021/05/13/republicans-seek-stop-schools-teaching-critical-race-theory/4993370001//.

357   Adam Lueke and Bryan Gibson, "Brief Mindfulness Meditation Reduces Discriminatory Behavior," *Psychology of Consciousness: Theory, Research, and Practice* 3, (2016): 34.

358   Peter H. Huang, "Can Practicing Mindfulness Improve Lawyer Decision-Making, Ethics, and Leadership?" *Houston Law Review* 55, (2017): 63, 112-114.

359   Peter H. Huang and Kelly J. Poore, "Can You Hear Me Later and Believe Me Now? Behavioral Law and Economics of Chronic Repeated Ambient Acoustic Pollution Causing Noise-Induced (Hidden) Hearing Loss," *Southern California Review of Law and Social Justice* 29, (2020): 193, 263-265.

360   Huang, "Can You Hear Me," 269.

361   Alison Wood Brooks, "How to Talk Gooder: The Science (and Serendipity) of Conversation, Behavior Change for Good," presentation at the University of Pennsylvania, YouTube, May 7, 2021, https://youtu.be/LTrrd94QEdU.

362   Michael Yeomans, Maurice E. Schweitzer, and Alison Wood Brooks, "The Conversational Circumplex: Identifying, Prioritizing, and Pursuing Informational and Relational Motives in Conversation," *Current Opinions in Psychology* 44, (2022): 302.

363   Julien C. Mirivel, *The Art of Positive Communication: Theory and Practice*, (International Academic Publishers, 2014).

364 Julien C. Mirivel, "The Six Keys to Positive Communication," *Greater Good Magazine,* April 27, 2021, https://greatergood. berkeley.edu/profile/julien_mirivel.

365 John Staughton, "Why Do People Have Different Skin Colors?" *Science ABC,* January 18, 2021, https://www.scienceabc.com/ humans/melanin-pigment-definition-meaning-skin-color.html.

366 Staughton.

367 Martin Luther King Jr., Address at Cornell College, Mount Vernon, Iowa, October 15, 1962, available at https://news.cornellcollege. edu/dr-martin-luther-kings-visit-to-cornell-college/.

368 Issa Kohler-Hausmann, "Eddie Murphy and the Dangers of Counterfactual Causal Thinking About Detecting Racial Discrimination," *Northwestern University Law Review* 113, no. 5, (2019): 1163, 1168, https://scholarlycommons.law.northwestern. edu/nulr/vol113/iss5/6/.

369 Kohler-Hausmann, 1170.

370 Kohler-Hausmann, 1170.

371 Kohler-Hausmann, 1214.

372 Katy Milkman, *How To Change: The Science Of Getting From Where You Are To Where You Want To Be,* (Portfolio Press, 2021); Leidy Klotz, *Subtract: The Untapped Power of Less*, (Flatiron Books, 2021); Leidy Klotz et al., "Beyond Rationality in Engineering Design for Sustainability," *Nature Sustainability* 1, (2021): 225; Robert Livingston, *The Conversation: How Seeking and Speaking the Truth About Racism Can Radically Transform Individuals and Organizations*, (Currency Press, 2021); Robert Livingston, "How to Promote Racial Equity in the Workplace," *Harvard Business Review,* September-October 2020, https://hbr.org/2020/09/how-to-promote-racial-equity-in-the-workplace.

373 Frank Wu, "Why Vincent Chin Matters."

374 Thomas Gries, Veronika Müller, and John T. Jost, "The Market for Belief Systems: A Formal Model of Ideological Choice," *Psychological Inquiry* 33, (2022): 65.

375 Andras Molnar and George Loewenstein, "Ideologies Are Like Possessions," *Psychological Inquiry* 33, (2022): 65, 84-87.

376   Molnar, 84, 87.

377   Molnar, 85-87.

378   Dan Kahan, "Fixing the Communication Failure," *Nature* 463, (2010): 296-297.

379   Molnar, 87.

380   Annie Duke, *Quit: The Power of Knowing When to Walk Away*, (Portfolio, 2022).

381   Molnar, 85-86.

Bibliography

Aaker, Jennifer and Naomi Bagdonas. *Humor, Seriously: Why Humor Is a Secret Weapon in Business and Life (And How Anyone Can Harness It. Even You)*. Currency Press, 2021.

Abelson, Robert P. "Beliefs Are Like Possessions." *Journal for the Theory of Social Behaviour* 16, (1984): 223.

Abramitzky, Ran and Leah Boustan. *Streets of Gold: America's Untold Story of Immigrant Success*. PublicAffairs, 2022.

Acemoglu, Daron, Philippe Aghion, and Fabrizio Zilibotti. "Distance to Frontier, Selection and Economic Growth." *Journal of the European Economic Association,* (2006): 37-74.

Ad Council. "Fight the Virus. Fight the Bias. Love Has No Labels." YouTube, July 21, 2020. https://youtu.be/5ocfEGYD_Xw.

Adichie, Chimamanda Ngozi. "The Danger of a Single Story," TEDGlobal, 2009. https://www.ted.com/talks/chimamanda_ngozi_adichie_the_danger_of_a_single_story.

Akerlof, George A. and Janet L. Yellen. "The Fair Wage Effort Hypothesis and Unemployment." *The Quarterly Journal of Economics* 105, (1990): 255.

Akerlof, George A. and Rachel E. Kranton. "Economics and Identity." *The Quarterly Journal of Economics* 115, (2000): 715.

Allem, Jon-Patrick. "Social Media Fuels Wave of Coronavirus Misinformation as Users Focus on Popularity, Not Accuracy." *The Conversation,* April 6, 2020. https://theconversation.com/social-media-fuels-wave-of-coronavirus-misinformation-as-users-focus-on-popularity-not-accuracy-135179.

Allison, Natalie. "Tennessee Republicans Want to Block Lessons on Systemic Racism in Schools." *USA Today*, May 3, 2021. https://www. usatoday.com/story/news/nation/2021/05/03/tennessee-republicans-take-critical-race-theory-lessons/4921671001/.

Allport, Gordon W. *The Nature of Prejudice*. Basic Books, 1979.

American Broadcasting Company. "Search Continues in Brutal Manhattan Attack on Asian Woman Heading to Church." Channel 7, New York, March 30, 2021. https://abc7ny.com/search-continues-in-brutal-nyc-attack-on-asian-woman-heading-to-church/10459000/.

Anderson, John P. et al. "Social Media, Securities Markets, and Expressive Trading." *Lewis and Clark Law Review* 25, (2022): 1223.

Anne Frank House. "Hitler's Antisemitism. Why Did He Hate the Jews?" https://www.annefrank.org/en/anne-frank/go-in-depth/why-did-hitler-hate-jews/.

Anti-Defamation League. "Reports of Anti-Asian Assaults, Harassment and Hate Crimes Rise as Coronavirus Spreads." American Defamation League Blog, July 18, 2020. https://www.adl.org/blog/reports-of-anti-asian-assaults-harassment-and-hate-crimes-rise-as-coronavirus-spreads.

Arithmetic of Compassion, website, https://arithmeticofcompassion.org/.

Arrow, Kenneth J. "I Know a Hawk from a Handsaw." In *Eminent Economists: Their Life Philosophies*. Edited by Michael Szenberg. Cambridge University Press, 1993.

Arrow, Kenneth J. "Some Mathematical Models of Race in the Labor Market." In *Racial Discrimination on Economic Life*, edited by A. H. Pascal. Lexington Books, 1972.

Arrow, Kenneth J. "Theory of Discrimination." In *Discrimination in Labor Markets*, edited by Orley Ashenfelter and Albert Rees. Princeton University Press, 1973.

Arrow, Kenneth J. "What Has Economics to Say About Racial Discrimination?" *Journal of Economic Perspectives,* (Spring 1998): 91.

Arrow, Kenneth J. In *Creating a Learning Society: A New Approach to Growth, Development, and Social Progress*. By Joseph E. Stiglitz and Bruce C. Greenwald. Columbia University Press, 2014.

Arrow, Kenneth J. *The Economics of Information, Volume 4.* Belknap Press, 1984.

Arrow, Kenneth J. *The Limits of Organization.* W. W. Norton, 1974.

Asakawa, Gil. "Jeff Yang in WSJ Deconstructs 'Model Minority' and 'New Jews' Stereotypes of Asian Americans." Nikkei View: The Asian American Blog, October 30, 2012. https://nikkeiview.com/blog/2012/10/jeff-yang-in-wsj-deconstructs-model-minority-new-jews-stereotypes-asian-americans.

Asher, Dana Bilsky. "The Surprising Link Between Laughter and Learning." *Fast Company,* May 10, 2016. https://www.fastcompany.com/3059651/the-surprising-link-between-laughter-and-learning.

Associated Press. "Georgia Court Throws Out Hate Crimes Law." *NBC News,* October 25, 2004. https://www.nbcnews.com/id/wbna6331341.

Association of Asian American Studies. "AAAS Statement on Anti-Asian Harassment and the Novel Coronavirus/Covid-19." March 5, 2020. https://aaastudies.org/aaas-statement-on-anti-asian-harassment-and-the-novel-coronavirus-covid-19/.

Ayu, Ariana. "The Enormous Cost of Unhappy Employees." *Inc.,* August 27, 2014. https://www.inc.com/ariana-ayu/the-enormous-cost-of-unhappy-employees.html.

Azar, Ofer H. "The Influence of Psychological Game Theory." *Games and Economic Behavior* 167, (2019): 459.

Baer, Stephanie K. "'The Cop Who Said the Spa Shooter Had a 'Bad Day' Previously Posted a Racist Shirt Blaming China for the Pandemic." *BuzzFeed News,* March 17, 2021. https://www.buzzfeednews.com/article/skbaer/spa-shooter-bad-day-racist-facebook (showing the Facebook post photo).

Baker, Peter. "A Half-Century After Wallace, Trump Echoes the Politics of Division." *The New York Times,* July 30, 2020. https://www.nytimes.com/2020/07/30/us/politics/trump-wallace.html.

Banks, Ralph Richard et al. *Racial Justice and Law: Cases and Materials.* Foundation Press, 2016.

Banks, Ralph Richard. "Beyond Colorblindness: Neo-Racialism and the Future of Race and Law Scholarship." *Harvard Blackletter Law Journal* 25, (2009): 41.

Baragona, Justin. "Trump Addresses 'Kung-Flu' Remark, Says Asian-Americans Agree '100 Percent' with Him Using 'Chinese Virus.'" *Daily Beast,* March 18, 2020. https://www.thedailybeast.com/trump-addresses-kung-flu-remark-says-asian-americans-agree-100-with-him-using-chinese-virus.

Bardella, Kurt. "'China Virus' Redux: For Trump and Republicans, It's Open Season on Asian Americans Like Me." *USA Today,* March 17, 2021. https://www.usatoday.com/story/opinion/2021/03/04/covid-racism-asian-americans-trump-provocations-column/6904348002/.

Battigalli, Pierpaolo and Martin Dufwenberg. "Belief-Dependent Motivations and Psychological Game Theory." *Journal of Economic Literature* 60, (2022): 833-882.

Baumol, William J. et al. *Contestable Markets and the Theory of Industry Structure.* Harcourt College Press, 1982.

Becker, Gary. *A Treatise on the Family.* Harvard University Press, 1993.

Bellafante, Ginia. "Private Schools Brought in Diversity Consultants. Outrage Ensued." *The New York Times,* April 23, 2021. https://www.nytimes.com/2021/04/23/nyregion/private-schools-diversity-brearley-dalton-grace.html.

Blascovich, Jim et al. "Perceiver Threat in Social Interactions with Stigmatized Others." *Journal of Personality and Social Psychology* 80, (2001): 253.

Blow, Charles M. "Is America a Racist Country?" *The New York Times,* May 2, 2021. https://www.nytimes.com/2021/05/02/opinion/america-racism.html.

Bodner, Ronit and Drazen Prelec. "Self-Signaling and Diagnostic Utility in Everyday Decision Making." In *The Psychology of Economic Decisions, Volume 1: Rationality and Well-Being.* Edited by Isabelle Brocas and Juab D. Carrillo. Oxford University Press, 2003.

Bogel-Burroughs, Nicolas. "Atlanta Spa Shootings Were Hate Crimes, Prosecutor Says." *The New York Times,* May 11, 2021. https://www.nytimes.com/2021/05/11/us/atlanta-spa-shootings-hate-crimes.html.

Bonilla-Silva, Eduardo. "Feeling Race: Theorizing the Racial Economy of Emotions." *American Sociological Review* 84, (2019): 1-2.

Botts v. State, 604 S.E.2d 512, 514 (2004).

Brax, David. "Motives, Reasons, and Responsibility in Hate/Bias Crime Legislation." *Criminal Justice Ethics* 35, (2016): 230.

Brock, William A. "Contestable Markets and the Theory of Industry Structure: A Review Article." *Journal of Political Economy* 91, (1983): 1055.

Brooks, Alison Wood. "How to Talk Gooder: The Science (and Serendipity) of Conversation, Behavior Change for Good." Presentation at the University of Pennsylvania. YouTube, May 7, 2021. https://youtu.be/LTrrd94QEdU.

Brooks, Thomas D. "First Amendment Penalty Enhancement for Hate Crimes: Content Regulation, Questionable State Interests and Non-Traditional Sentencing." *Journal of Criminal Law and Criminology* 84, (1994): 703.

Bunch III, Lonnie G. "We Are American, and We Stand Together: Asian American Resilience, Belonging and Justice." Remarks at the Smithsonian Asian Pacific American Center. May 15, 2021. YouTube, https://youtu.be/Lm0T-EQluiU.

Cai, Weiyi et al. "Swelling Anti-Asian Violence: Who Is Being Attacked Where." *The New York Times,* April 3, 2021. https://www.nytimes.com/interactive/2021/04/03/us/anti-asian-attacks.html.

Cameron, Samuel. "Widening the Economic Approach to Hatred." *Forum for Social Economics* 39, (2009): 19.

Cameron, Samuel. *The Economics of Hate.* Edward Elgar Publishing, 2009.

Cantrell, Deborah. "Exploring Transformative Silence and Protest." *Rutgers Journal of Law and Religion* 22, (2021): 83.

Cantu, Edward and Lee Jussim. "Microaggressions, Questionable Science, and Free Speech." *Texas Review of Law and Politics* 26, (2021): 217.

Chang, Gordon H. and Shelley Fisher Fishkin. "Geography of Chinese Workers Building the Transcontinental Railroad." Chinese Railroad Workers in North America Project, Stanford University, 2018, https://web.stanford.edu/group/chineserailroad/cgi-bin/website/virtual/.

Chaplinsky v. New Hampshire, 315 U.S. 568, 572 (1942).

Chapman, Gary. *The 5 Love Languages: The Secret to Love that Lasts.* Northfield Publishing, 2015.

Charles, Dan. "Heisenberg's Principles Kept Bomb from Nazis." *New Scientist,* September 5, 1992. https://www.newscientist.com/article/mg13518370-300-heisenbergs-principles-kept-bomb-from-nazis/.

Chen, Brian X. "There Is No Rung on the Ladder That Protects You from Hate." *The New York Times*, March 24, 2021. https://www.nytimes.com/2021/03/20/technology/personaltech/asian-american-wealth-gap.html.

Chia, Jessica. "Keys, Wallet, Pepper Spray: The New Reality for Asian-Americans." *The New York Times,* May 20, 2021. https://www.nytimes.com/2021/05/20/nyregion/asian-americans-attacks-nyc.html.

Chichilnisky, Graciela. "Sex and the Ivy League." In *Reflections of Eminent Economists,* edited by Michael Szenberg and Lall Ramrattan. Edward Elgar Publishers, 2004.

Chinese Exclusion Act, Pub. L. No. 47-126, 126, 22 Stat. 58 (1882).

Cho, John. "Coronavirus Reminds Asian Americans Like Me That Our Belonging is Conditional." *Los Angeles Times,* April 22, 2020. https://www.latimes.com/opinion/story/2020-04-22/asian-american-discrimination-john-cho-coronavirus.

Chow, Kat. "If We Called Ourselves Yellow." NPR. September 27, 2018. https://www.npr.org/sections/codeswitch/2018/09/27/647989652/if-we-called-ourselves-yellow.

Chow, Serena. "The Mental Health Implications of Covid-19 Related Violence Against Asian Americans." *Asian American News,* April 30, 2020. https://asamnews.com/2020/04/30/rise-in-anti-asian-hate-crimes-expected-to-adversely-impact-mental-health-of-asian-americans/.

Chuang, Angie. "Two Stereotypes that Diminish the Humanity of the Atlanta Shooting Victims—and All Asian Americans." *The Conversation,* March 26, 2021. https://theconversation.com/two-stereotypes-that-diminish-the-humanity-of-the-atlanta-shooting-victims-and-all-asian-americans-157762.

Chung, Jamison et al. "Combating AAPI Hate." *The Regulatory Review,* May 8, 2021. https://www.theregreview.org/2021/05/08/saturday-seminar-combating-aapi-hate/.

Cohen, Max. "Kellyanne Conway Reacts to Trump's Use of 'Kung Flu,' Months After Calling Term 'Highly Offensive.'" *Politico,* June 24, 2020. https://www.politico.com/news/2020/06/24/kellyanne-conway-trump-kung-flu-coronavirus-337682.

Coy, Peter. "Why So Many Children of Immigrants Rise to the Top." *The New York Times,* July 11, 2022. https://www.nytimes.com/interactive/2022/07/11/opinion/immigrants-success-america.html.

Cummings, Judith. "Detroit Asian-Americans Protest Lenient Penalties for Murder." *The New York Times,* April 26, 1983. https://www.nytimes.com/1983/04/26/us/detroit-asian-americans-protest-lenient-penalties-for-murder.html.

DeAngelis, Tori. "Unmasking 'Racial Microaggressions.'" *Monitor* 40, (2009): 42, https://www.apa.org/monitor/2009/02/microaggression.

Dell, Natalya. "Intersecting Axes of Privilege, Domination, and Oppression." Natalyad (website). February 10, 2014. https://sites.google.com/site/natalyadell/home/intersectionality.

Denrell, Jerker. "The Hot Stove Effect." https://sites.google.com/site/jerkerdenrell/hot-stove-effect.

Densho. "Preserving Japanese American Stories of the Past for the Generations of Tomorrow." https://densho.org.

Dismantling Racism. *Racism Defined.* https://www.dismantlingracism.org/racism-defined.html.

Duke, Annie. *Quit: The Power of Knowing When to Walk Away.* Portfolio, 2022.

Editorial Board. "Asian-Americans Are Scared for a Reason." *The New York Times,* March 18, 2021. https://www.nytimes.com/2021/03/18/opinion/anti-asian-american-violence.html.

Editorial Staff, "Hate Crimes Against Asian Americans Are at an 'Alarming Level,' UN Says." NextShark, October 20, 2020. https://nextshark.com/un-experts-trump-attacks-against-asian-americans/.

Editorial Staff. "Ahmaud Arbery Shooting: A Timeline of the Case." *The New York Times*, April 19, 2021. https://www.nytimes.com/article/ahmaud-arbery-timeline.html.

Editorial Staff. "Clinton on Implicit Bias in Policing." *The Washington Post*, September 26, 2016. https://www.washingtonpost.com/video/politics/clinton-on-implicit-bias-in-policing/2016/09/26/46e1e88c-8441-11e6-b57d-dd49277af02f_video.html.

Edmondson, Catie and Jim Tankersley. "Biden is Set to Sign a Bill Addressing Hate Crimes Against Asian-Americans." *The New York Times*, May 20, 2021. https://www.nytimes.com/2021/05/20/us/politics/biden-asian-hate-crimes.html.

Edmondson, Catie. "Asian-American Lawmakers Call Out Racist Language: 'I Am Not a Virus.'" *The New York Times,* March 18, 2021. https://www.nytimes.com/2021/03/18/us/politics/asian-politicians-racism.html.

Edmondson, Catie. "House Democrats Hold a Rare Congressional Hearing on Anti-Asian Discrimination." *The New York Times*, March 18, 2021. https://www.nytimes.com/2021/03/18/us/congress-hearing-asian-american-discrimination.html.

Edmondson, Catie. "Senate Resoundingly Passes Bill to Target Anti-Asian Hate Crimes." *The New York Times*, April 22, 2021. https://www.nytimes.com/2021/04/22/us/politics/senate-anti-asian-hate-crimes.html.

Eisenberg, Daniel et al. Healthy Minds Network. "The Healthy Minds Study: Fall 2020 Data Report," Fall 2020. https://healthymindsnetwork.org/wp-content/uploads/2021/02/HMS-Fall-2020-National-Data-Report.pdf.

Eisgruber, Christopher L. "Letter from President Eisgruber on the University's Efforts to Combat Systemic Racism." Princeton University, September 2, 2020. https://www.princeton.edu/news/2020/09/02/letter-president-eisgruber-universitys-efforts-combat-systemic-racism.

Ekman, Eve and Jeremy Adam Smith. "When Racism Makes Us Sick." In *Are We Born Racist? New Insights from Neuroscience and Positive Psychology*. Edited by Jason Marsh et al. Beacon Press, 2010.

Elliott, Jane. *A Collar in My Pocket: Blue Eyes/Brown Eyes Exercise*. Self-Published, 2016.

Embrace Race. https://www.embracerace.org/.

Fader, Susan. "Narrative Economics: Reframing the Roles of Storytelling and Behavioral Economics." *Qualitative Research Consultants Association Views,* July 16, 2020. https://qrcaviews. org/2020/07/16/narrative-economics-reframing-the-roles-of-storytelling-and-behavioral-economics/.

Fallon, Jimmy. "Jane Elliott on Her 'Blue Eyes/Brown Eyes Exercise' and Fighting Racism." *The Tonight Show.* YouTube, June 2, 2020. https://youtu.be/f2z-ahJ4uws.

Fang, Jenn. "Andrew Yang Is Wrong: Respectability Politics Won't Save Asian Americans from Racist Violence." *Reappropriate,* April 2, 2020. http://reappropriate.co/2020/04/andrew-yang-is-wrong-respectability-politics-wont-save-asian-americans-from-racist-violence/.

Fausset, Richard and Neil Vigdor. "8 People Killed in Atlanta-Area Massage Parlor Shootings." *The New York Times*, March 16, 2021. https://www.nytimes.com/2021/03/16/us/atlanta-shootings-massage-parlor.html.

Federal Bureau of Investigation. "2019 Hate Crime Statistics." Uniform Crime Reporting Program. https://ucr.fbi.gov/hate-crime/2019/topic-pages/incidents-and-offenses.

Federal Bureau of Investigation. "Hate Crimes." https://www.fbi.gov/investigate/civil-rights/hate-crimes.

Ford, Thomas E. et al. "More Than 'Just a Joke': The Prejudice-Releasing Function of Sexist Humor." *Personality and Social Psychology Bulletin* 34, (2008): 159.

Friedersdorf, Conor. "Why Critics of the 'Microaggressions' Framework Are Skeptical." *The Atlantic,* September 4, 2015. https://www.theatlantic.com/politics/archive/2015/09/why-critics-of-the-microaggressions-framework-are-skeptical/405106/.

Frimodig, Gabriel. "Fear Leads to Anger, Anger Leads to Hate, Hate to Suffering." YouTube, July 15, 2020. https://www.youtube.com/watch?v=kFnFr-DOPf8.

Gale, Lewis R. et al. "An Economic Analysis of Hate Crime." *Eastern Economic Journal* 28, (2002): 203.

Garcia, Sandra E. "Where Did BIPOC Come From?" *The New York Times*, June 17, 2020. https://www.nytimes.com/article/what-is-bipoc.html.

Geanakoplos, John et al. "Psychological Games and Sequential Rationality." *Games and Economic Behavior* 1, (1989): 60.

Geronimus, Arline T. et al. "Do US Black Women Experience Stress-Related Accelerated Biological Aging? A Novel Theory and First Population-Based Test of Black-White Differences in Telomere Length." *Human Nature* 21, (2010): 19.

Gerstmann, Evan. "Irony: Hate Crimes Surge Against Asian Americans While They Are on the Front Lines Fighting Covid-19." *Forbes*, April 4, 2020. https://www.forbes.com/sites/evangerstmann/2020/04/04/irony-hate-crimes-surge-against-asian-americans-while-they-are-on-the-front-lines-fighting-covid-19/#7963c8a03b70.

Gibbs, Michael. "Job Design, Learning and Intrinsic Motivation." University of Chicago Booth School of Business. Working Paper No. 21-11. April 11, 2021. https://papers.ssrn.com/sol3/papers.cfm?abstract_id=3824874.

Gibson, Charlotte. "UCLA's Natalie Chou Won't Stand for Anti-Asian Racism Related to Coronavirus." ESPN, March 26, 2020. https://www.espn.com/espnw/voices/story/_/id/28955666/ucla-natalie-chou-stand-anti-asian-racism-related-coronavirus.

Glaeser, Edward L. "The Political Economy of Hatred." *Quarterly Journal of Economics* 120, (2005): 45.

Glass, Leon. "A Topological Theorem for Nonlinear Dynamics in Chemical and Ecological Networks." *Proceedings of the National Academy of Sciences* 72, (1975).

Gottman, John et al. *The Mathematics of Marriage: Dynamic Nonlinear Models.* Bradford, 2005.

Greenwald, Anthony G. and Linda Hamilton Krieger. "Implicit Bias: Scientific Foundations." *California Law Review* 94, (2006): 945, 955-956.

Gries, Thomas, Veronika Müller and John T. Jost. "The Market for Belief Systems: A Formal Model of Ideological Choice." *Psychological Inquiry* 33, (2022): 65.

Griffin, John Howard. *Black Like Me*. Berkley, 2010.

Gstalter, Morgan. "WHO Official Warns Against Calling It 'Chinese Virus,' Says 'There's No Blame in This.'" *The Hill,* March 19, 2020. https://thehill.com/homenews/administration/488479-who-official-warns-against-calling-it-chinese-virus-says-there-is-no.

Guan, Nancy. "'We Need Protection': Georgia State Sen. Michelle Au Warned of Anti-Asian Violence Before Atlanta Shootings." *USA Today,* March 20, 2021. https://www.usatoday.com/story/news/nation/2021/03/20/atlanta-shooting-state-sen-michelle-au-condemns-anti-asian-violence/4781935001/.

Guo, Jeff. "The Real Reasons the U.S. Became Less Racist Toward Asian Americans." *The Washington Post,* November 29, 2016. https://www.washingtonpost.com/news/wonk/wp/2016/11/29/the-real-reason-americans-stopped-spitting-on-asian-americans-and-started-praising-them/.

Gupta, Alisha Haridasani. "A Teacher Held a Famous Racism Exercise in 1968. She's Still at It." *The New York Times*, July 15, 2020. https://www.nytimes.com/2020/07/04/us/jane-elliott-anti-racism-blue-eyes-brown-eyes.html.

Hansen, Claire. "What is a Hate Crime?" *U.S. News and World Report,* April 27, 2021. https://www.usnews.com/news/national-news/articles/what-is-a-hate-crime.

Harrison, Isheka N. "7 Things to Know About Howard University Economist William Spriggs." Moguldom Nation, October 12, 2020. https://moguldom.com/310025/7-things-to-know-about-howard-university-economist-william-spriggs/.

Heller, Steven. "The Artistic History of American Anti-Asian Racism." *The Atlantic,* February 20, 2014. https://www.theatlantic.com/entertainment/archive/2014/02/the-artistic-history-of-american-anti-asian-racism/283962/.

Hertwig, Ralph and Christoph Engel, eds. *Deliberate Ignorance: Choosing Not to Know.* MIT Press, 2021.

Hill, Claire A. "The Law and Economics of Identity." *Queen's Law Journal* 32, (2007): 389.

Hill, Kyle. "Was Yoda's Advice Any Good Psychologically?" *Discover,* May 6, 2014. https://www.discovermagazine.com/the-sciences/was-yodas-advice-any-good-psychologically.

Hirschman, Albert O. *Exit, Voice and Loyalty: Responses to Decline in Firms, Organizations, and States,* Harvard University Press, 1970.

Ho, Jennifer. "Anti-Asian Racism and Covid-19." *Colorado Arts and Science Magazine,* revised July 16, 2020. https://www.colorado.edu/asmagazine/2020/04/08/anti-asian-racism-and-covid-19.

Holmstrom, Bengt. "Moral Hazard in Teams." *The Bell Journal of Economics* 13, (1982): 324.

Holt, Brianna. "The Return of Jane Elliott." *The New York Times*, July 24, 2020. https://www.nytimes.com/2020/07/15/style/jane-elliott-anti-racism.html.

Hong, Cathy Park. "The Slur I Never Expected to Hear in 2020." *The New York Times,* April 12, 2020. https://www.nytimes.com/2020/04/12/magazine/asian-american-discrimination-coronavirus.html.

Hong, Nicole and Jonah E. Bromwich. "Asian-Americans Are Being Attacked. Why Are Hate Crime Charges So Rare?" *The New York Times,* October 26, 2021. https://www.nytimes.com/2021/03/18/nyregion/asian-hate-crimes.html.

Hong, Nicole et al. "Brutal Attack on Filipino Woman Sparks Outrage: 'Everybody Is on Edge.'" *The New York Times,* April 6, 2021. https://www.nytimes.com/2021/03/30/nyregion/asian-attack-nyc.html.

Hoption, Colette et al. "It's Not You, It's Me: Transformational Leadership and Self-Deprecating Humor." *Leadership and Organizational Development Journal* 34, (2013): 4.

House Committee on the Judiciary. "Discrimination and Violence Against Asian Americans." YouTube, March 18, 2021. https://youtu.be/547JYf-VA_Q.

Howard University School of Law. "Social Justice: Implicit Bias and Microaggressions." https://library.law.howard.edu/socialjustice/bias.

Hsu, Tiffany. "A New P.S.A. Hopes to Put a Focus on Pandemic-Related Racism." *The New York Times*, July 21, 2020. https://www.nytimes.com/2020/07/21/business/a-new-psa-hopes-to-put-a-focus-on-pandemic-related-racism.html.

Hsu, Tiffany. "Anti-Asian Harassment Is Surging. Can Ads and Hashtags Help?" *The New York Times*, July 21, 2020. https://www.nytimes.com/2020/07/21/business/media/asian-american-harassment-ad-council.html.

Hswen, Yulin et al. "Association of '#covid19' Versus '#chinesevirus' with Anti-Asian Sentiments on Twitter: March 9–23, 2020." *American Journal of Public Health* 111, no. 5, (2021): 956. https://www.crmvet.org/docs/otheram.htm.

Hua, Vanessa. "In a Role Reversal, Asian-Americans Aim to Protect Their Parents from Hate." *The New York Times,* March 29, 2021. https://www.nytimes.com/2021/03/26/well/family/asian-american-hate-racism.html.

Huang, Justin T., Masha Krupenkin, David Rothschild, and Julia Lee Cunningham. "The Cost of Anti-Asian Racism During the COVID-19 Pandemic." *Nature Human Behavior,* (2023). https://doi.org/10.1038/s41562-022-01493-6.

Huang, Peter H. "Book Review of *Why the Law Is So Perverse.*" *Journal of Legal Education* 63, (2013): 131, 138-48, https://jle.aals.org/home/vol63/iss1/9/.

Huang, Peter H. "Can Practicing Mindfulness Improve Lawyer Decision-Making, Ethics, and Leadership?" *Houston Law Review* 55, (2017): 63, 112-114.

Huang, Peter H. "Dangers of Monetary Commensurability: A Psychological Game Model of Contagion." *University of Pennsylvania Law Review* 146, (1998): 1701.

Huang, Peter H. "Emotional Reactions to Law and Economics, Market Metaphors, and Rationality Rhetoric." In *Theoretical Foundations of Law and Economics.* Edited by Mark D. White. Cambridge University Press, 2008.

Huang, Peter H. "Pandemic Emotions: The Good, the Bad, and the Unconscious—Implications for Public Health, Financial Economics, Law, and Leadership." *Northwestern Journal of Law and Social Policy* 16, (2021): 80, 127-29.

Huang, Peter H. "Structural Stability of Financial and Accounting Signaling Equilibria." *Research in Finance* 9, (1991): 37-47.

Huang, Peter H. and Ho-Mou Wu. "Emotional Responses in Litigation." *International Review of Law and Economics* 12, (1992): 31.

Huang, Peter H. and Ho-Mou Wu. "More Order Without More Law: A Theory of Social Norms and Organizational Cultures." *Journal of Law, Economics, and Organization* 10, (1992): 390, 394.

Huang, Peter H. and Kelly J. Poore. "Can You Hear Me Later and Believe Me Now? Behavioral Law and Economics of Chronic Repeated Ambient Acoustic Pollution Causing Noise-Induced (Hidden) Hearing Loss." *Southern California Review of Law and Social Justice* 29, (2020): 193, 263-265.

Hung, Louise. "35 Years After Vincent Chin's Brutal Murder, Nothing Has Changed." *Global Comment,* June 28, 2017. https://globalcomment.com/35-years-vincent-chins-brutal-murder-nothing-changed/.

Hurd, Heidi M. "Why Liberals Should Hate 'Hate Crime Legislation.'" *Law and Philosophy* 20, (2001): 215.

Hurd, Heidi M. and Michael S. Moore. "Punishing Hatred and Prejudice." *Stanford Law Review* 56, (2004).

Jaffe, David, Katherine Bender, and Jerome M. Organ. "It is Okay to Not Be Okay: The 2021 Survey of Law Student Well-Being." *University of Louisville Law Review* 60, no. 3, (2022): 439, 467. https://uofllawreview.org/online-edition.

Jan, Tracy. "As They Fight Virus, Asian Americans Battle Racism." *The Washington Post,* May 22, 2020.

Jan, Tracy. "Asian American Doctors and Nurses Are Fighting Racism and the Coronavirus." *The Washington Post*, May 19, 2020. https://www.washingtonpost.com/business/2020/05/19/asian-american-discrimination/.

Johnson, Stefanie K. "Is Covid-19 Increasing Racially Motivated Crimes?" *Psychology Today,* May 22, 2020. https://www.psychologytoday.com/us/blog/stand-out-and-fit-in/202005/is-covid-19-increasing-racially-motivated-crimes.

Jung, John. *Chopsticks in the Land of Cotton: Lives of Mississippi Delta Chinese Grocers.* Yin and Yang Press, 2008.

Kahan, Dan M. "Two Liberal Fallacies in the Hate Crimes Debate." *Law and Philosophy* 20, (2001): 175, 183-185.

Kahan, Dan. "Fixing the Communication Failure." *Nature* 463, (2010): 296-297.

Kahn, Jonathan. *Race on the Brain: What Implicit Racism Gets Wrong About the Struggle for Racial Justice.* Colombia University Press, 2017.

Kao, Audiey. "Interview with Jennifer Ho." University of Colorado, Boulder, June 2020. https://journalofethics.ama-assn.org/videocast/ethics-talk-spread-anti-asian-racism-and-xenophobia-during-covid-19-pandemic.

Kashdan, Todd B. "The Science Behind Holding Your Identity(s) Loosely." The Growth Equation (website). https://thegrowtheq.com/the-science-behind-holding-your-identitys-loosely/.

Kim, Juliana. "Constance Wu's Reveal Speaks to the Profound Pressure Asian American Women Face." National Public Radio, July 18, 2022. https://www.npr.org/2022/07/18/1112055817/constance-wu-asian-american-women.

Kim, Regina. "Atlanta Spa Shootings: What Korean-Language Media Told Us That the Mainstream Media Didn't." *Rolling Stone,* March 31, 2021. https://www.rollingstone.com/culture/culture-news/atlanta-shootings-what-korean-language-media-told-us-that-the-mainstream-media-didnt-1149698/.

King Jr., Martin Luther. Address at Cornell College. October 15, 1962. https://news.cornellcollege.edu/dr-martin-luther-kings-visit-to-cornell-college/.

King Jr., Martin Luther. Speech at Western Michigan University, December 18, 1963. https://libguides.wmich.edu/mlkatwmu/speech.

King Jr., Martin Luther. "The Other America." Speech delivered on April 14, 1967.

Klainerman, Sergiu. "Princeton's President Is Wrong. The University Is Not Systemically Racist." *Newsweek,* September 9, 2020. https://www.newsweek.com/princetons-president-wrong-university-not-systemically-racist-opinion-1530480.

Klotz, Leidy et al. "Beyond Rationality in Engineering Design for Sustainability." *Nature Sustainability* 1, (2021): 225.

Klotz, Leidy. *Subtract: The Untapped Power of Less.* Flatiron Books, 2021.

Knowles, Hannah and Haisten Willis. "Prosecutor to Seek Hate-Crime Charges Against White Man Accused in Atlanta-Area Spa Killings." *The Washington Post,* May 11, 2021.

Koetse, Manya. "Chinese Reporter Who Cried on Air over Abe's Death Attempted Suicide after Online Backlash." What's on Weibo, July 21, 2022, https://www.whatsonweibo.com/chinese-reporter-who-cried-on-air-over-abes-death-attempted-suicide-after-online-backlash/.

Koetse, Manye. Twitter, July 8, 2022. https://twitter.com/manyapan/status/1545386635008921600.

Kohler-Hausmann, Issa. "Eddie Murphy and the Dangers of Counterfactual Causal Thinking About Detecting Racial Discrimination." *Northwestern University Law Review* 113, no. 5, (2019): 1163, 1168, https://scholarlycommons.law.northwestern.edu/nulr/vol113/iss5/6/.

Kolhatkar, Sheelah. "Robinhood's Big Gamble." *The New Yorker,* May 17, 2021. https://www.newyorker.com/magazine/2021/05/17/robinhoods-big-gamble.

Kopecki, Dawn. "WHO Officials Warn US President Trump Against Calling Coronavirus 'the Chinese Virus.'" CNBC, March 18, 2020. https://www.cnbc.com/2020/03/18/who-officials-warn-us-president-trump-against-calling-coronavirus-the-chinese-virus.html.

Kraus, George. "Chinese Laborers and the Construction of the Central Pacific." *Utah Historical Quarterly* 37, (1969): 41-42.

Kristof, Nicholas. "To Beat Trump, Mock Him." *The New York Times,* September 26, 2020. https://www.nytimes.com/2020/09/26/opinion/sunday/trump-politics-humor.html.

Kupferschmidt, Kai. "Discovered a Disease? WHO Has New Rules for Avoiding Offensive Names." *Science Insider,* May 11, 2015. https://www.sciencemag.org/news/2015/05/discovered-disease-who-has-new-rules-avoiding-offensive-names.

Lam, Larissa and Baldwin Chiu. *Far East Deep South,* 2020, https://fareastdeepsouth.com/.

Lang, Cady. "Hate Crimes Against Asian Americans Are on the Rise. Many Say More Policing Isn't the Answer." *Time,* February 18, 2021. https://time.com/5938482/asian-american-attacks/.

LeBoeuf, Robyn A. et al. "The Conflicting Choices of Alternating Selves." *Organizational Behavior and Human Decision Processes* 111, (2010): 48, 52.

Lee, Gregory B. "Dirty, Diseased and Demented: The Irish, the Chinese, and Racist Representation." *Journal of Global Cultural Studies* 31, no. 5, (2017): 6.

Lee, Jennifer and Min Zhou. *The Asian American Achievement Paradox.* Russell Sage Foundation, 2015.

Lee, Robert G. "The Cold War Origins of the Model Minority Myth." In *Asian American Studies Now: A Critical Reader.* Edited by Jean Yu-wen Shen Wu and Thomas C. Chen. Rutgers University Press, 2010.

Lehmann-Willenbrock, Nale and Joseph A. Allen. "How Fun Are Your Meetings? Investigating the Relationship Between Humor Patterns in Team Interactions and Team Performance." *Journal of Applied Psychology* 99, (2014): 1278.

Leong, Nancy. "Racial Capitalism." *Harvard University Law Review* 126, (2013): 2151-2226. https://harvardlawreview.org/2013/06/racial-capitalism/.

Leong, Nancy. "The Misuse of Asian Americans in the Affirmative Action Debate." *University of California Los Angeles Law Review,* May 23, 2016. https://www.uclalawreview.org/misuse-asian-americans-affirmative-action-debate/.

Leong, Nancy. *Identity Capitalists: The Powerful Insiders Who Exploit Diversity to Maintain Inequality.* Stanford University Press, 2021.

Letendre, Kenneth et al. "Does Infectious Disease Cause Global Variation in the Frequency of Intrastate Armed Conflict and Civil War?" *Biological Review* 85, no. 3, (2010): 669.

Lew-Williams, Beth. *The Chinese Must Go: Violence, Exclusion, and the Making of the Alien in America.* Harvard University Press, 2021.

Lilienfeld, Scott O. "Microaggressions: Strong Claims, Inadequate Evidence." *Perspectives on Psychological Science* 12, (2017): 138.

Linville, Patricia W. "Self-Complexity and Affective Extremity: Don't Put All of Your Eggs in One Cognitive Basket." *Social Cognition* 3, (1985): 94-120.

Linville, Patricia W. "Self-Complexity as a Cognitive Buffer Against Stress-Related Illness and Depression." *Journal of Personality and Social Psychology* 52, (1987): 663–667.

Little, Becky. "How the 1982 Murder of Vincent Chin Ignited a Push for Asian American Rights." History Channel, May 5, 2020. https://www.history.com/news/vincent-chin-murder-asian-american-rights.

Liu, Roseann. "Dismantling the Barrier Between Asians and African Americans." *The Philadelphia Inquirer,* June 8, 2018. https://www.inquirer.com/philly/opinion/stop-and-go-asian-african-americans-20180608.html.

Liu, Simu. Twitter, April 2, 2020. https://twitter.com/SimuLiu/status/1245886734337859584.

Livingston, Robert. "How to Promote Racial Equity in the Workplace." *Harvard Business Review,* September-October 2020. https://hbr.org/2020/09/how-to-promote-racial-equity-in-the-workplace.

Livingston, Robert. *The Conversation: How Seeking and Speaking the Truth About Racism Can Radically Transform Individuals and Organizations.* Currency Press, 2021.

Lo, Andrew W. and Ruixun Zhang. "The Wisdom of Crowds Versus the Madness of Mobs: An Evolutionary Model of Bias, Polarization, and Other Challenges to Collective Intelligence." *Collective Intelligence* 1, (2022): 1.

Loewenstein, George and Andras Molnar. "The Renaissance of Belief-Based Utility in Economics." *Nature Human Behavior* 2, (2018): 166.

Loewenstein, George. *Exotic Preferences: Behavioral Economics and Human Motivation.* Oxford University Press, 2008.

Lu, Yao, Neeraj Kaushal, Xiaoning Huang, and S. Michael Gaddis. "Priming Covid-19 Salience Increases Prejudice and Discriminatory Intent Against Asians and Hispanics." *Proceedings of the National Academy of Sciences* 118, (2021): e2105125118.

Lueke, Adam and Bryan Gibson. "Brief Mindfulness Meditation Reduces Discriminatory Behavior." *Psychology of Consciousness: Theory, Research, and Practice* 3, (2016): 34.

Lukianoff, Greg and Jonathan Haidt. *The Coddling of the American Mind: How Good Intentions and Bad Ideas Are Setting Up a Generation for Failure.* Penguin Press, 2018.

Luo, Benny. "Andrew Yang Responds to Backlash on *The Washington Post* Op-Ed," Nextshark, April 7, 2020.https://nextshark.com/andrew-yang-responds-washington-post-op-ed/.

Magnuson Act, Pub. L. No. 78-199, 57 Stat. 600 (1943).

Mallett, Robyn K. et al. "What Did He Mean by That? Humor Decreases Attributions of Sexism and Confrontation of Sexist Jokes." *Sex Roles* 75, (2016): 272.

Margolin, Josh. "FBI Warns of Potential Surge in Hate Crimes Against Asian Americans Amid Coronavirus." *ABC News,* March 27, 2020. https://abcnews.go.com/US/fbi-warns-potential-surge-hate-crimes-asian-americans/story?id=69831920.

Marsh, Shawn C. "The Lens of Implicit Bias." National Center for Juvenile Justice, 2009. https://www.ncjfcj.org/publications/the-lens-of-implicit-bias/.

Massachusetts General Hospital Center for Cross-Cultural Student Emotional Wellness. "Guide for Parents of Asian/Asian American Adolescents." https://www.mghstudentwellness.org/resources-1/guide-for-parents-of-asianasian-american-adolescents.

Massachusetts General Hospital Student Wellness. "Talking to Teens About Anti-Asian Discrimination in the Era of Covid-19: Guidance from Research and Practice." March 5, 2021. https://vimeo.com/520018357.

Matysik, Jerry. "Implicit Bias and Law Enforcement: Reducing Blame and Understanding the Brain." Lexipol. February 15, 2017. https://www.lexipol.com/resources/blog/implicit-bias-law-enforcement-reducing-blame-understanding-brain/.

McFarland, Sam. "Identification with All Humanity: The Antithesis of Prejudice, and More." In *Cambridge Handbook of the Psychology of Prejudice.* Cambridge University Press, 2018.

McGann-Bartleman, Daniel. "If You're a Bystander, You're a Racist." *The Breeze,* October 13, 2016. https://www.breezejmu.org/opinion/if-youre-a-bystander-youre-a-racist/article_d7d83444-90cc-11e6-870c-4b9e8554a534.html.

Mendes, Wendy Berry et al. "Why Egalitarianism Might Be Good for Your Health: Physiological Thriving During Stressful Intergroup Encounters." *Psychological Science* 18, (2007): 991.

Merica, Dan. "Hillary Clinton Talks Race: 'We All Have Implicit Biases.'" CNN. April 20, 2016. https://www.cnn.com/2016/04/20/politics/hillary-clinton-race-implicit-biases/index.html.

Milgrom, Paul and John D. Roberts. "Bargaining Costs, Influence Costs, and the Organization of Economic Activity." In *The Economic Nature of the Firm: A Reader.* Edited by Randall S. Kroszner and Louis Putterman. Cambridge University Press, 2014.

Milkman, Katy. *How To Change: The Science Of Getting From Where You Are To Where You Want To Be.* Portfolio Press, 2021.

Miller, Ryan W. "'Absolutely Disgusting and Outrageous': Elderly Asian American Woman Released from New York Hospital After Brutal Attack; Suspect Sought." *USA Today,* March 30, 2021. https://www.usatoday.com/story/news/nation/2021/03/30/nypd-asian-american-woman-assaulted/7057944002/.

Mirengoff, Paul. "Northwestern Law Dean Says He's a Racist." Power Line, November 1, 2020. https://www.powerlineblog.com/archives/2020/11/northwestern-law-dean-says-hes-a-racist.php.

Mirivel, Julien C. "The Six Keys to Positive Communication." *Greater Good Magazine,* April 27, 2021. https://greatergood.berkeley.edu/profile/julien_mirivel.

Mirivel, Julien C. *The Art of Positive Communication: Theory and Practice.* International Academic Publishers, 2014.

MIT Sloan School Office of Media Relations. "New Study Suggests Evolutionary Forces Are Behind Collective Discrimination." November 10, 2022. https://mitsloan.mit.edu/press/new-study-suggests-evolutionary-forces-are-behind-collective-discrimination.

Mitchell, Bruce and Juan Franco. "HOLC 'Redlining' Maps: The Persistent Structure of Segregation and Economic Inequality." National Community Reinvestment Coalition, March 20, 2018. https://ncrc.org/holc/.

Moffat, Mike. "The Economics of Discrimination: An Examination of the Economic Theory of Statistical Discrimination." ThoughtCo., April 10, 2019. https://www.thoughtco.com/the-economics-of-discrimination-1147202.

Molano, Sarah. "The Problem with Respectability Politics," *Pipe Dream,* April 23, 2018. https://www.bupipedream.com/opinions/94369/the-problem-with-respectability-politics/.

Molnar, Andras and George Loewenstein. "Ideologies Are Like Possessions." *Psychological Inquiry* 33, (2022): 65, 84-87.

Molnar, Andras and George Loewenstein. "Thoughts and Players: An Introduction to Old and New Economic Perspectives on Beliefs." In *The Cognitive Science of Beliefs: A Multidisciplinary Approach.* Edited by Julien Musolino. Cambridge University Press, 2022.

Most, Andrea. "'You've Got to be Carefully Taught': The Politics of Race in Rodgers and Hammerstein's *South Pacific.*" *Theatre Journal* 52, (2000): 307.

Mui, Vai-Lam. "The Economics of Envy." *Journal of Economic Behavior and Organization* 26, (1995): 311.

Mujcic, Redzo and Andrew J. Oswald. "Is Envy Harmful to a Society's Psychological Health and Wellbeing? Longitudinal Study of 18,000 Adults." *Social Science and Medicine* 198, (2018): 103.

National Center for State Courts. "Implicit Bias." https://www.ncsc.org/information-and-resources/racial-justice/implicit-bias.

National Committee on U.S.-China Relations. "The 'Model Minority' Myth: Jennifer Ho and Frank H. Wu." YouTube, August 6, 2020, https://youtu.be/zHFvEvPo5z0.

National Defense Authorization Act for Fiscal Year 2010, Pub. L. No. 111-84, 123 Stat. 2190.

National Initiative for Building Community Trust and Justice. "Implicit Bias." https://trustandjustice.org/resources/intervention/implicit-bias.

Natividad, Ivan. "Racist Harassment of Asian Health Care Workers Won't Cure Coronavirus." *Berkeley News,* April 9, 2020. https://news.berkeley.edu/2020/04/09/racist-harassment-of-asian-health-care-workers-wont-cure-coronavirus/.

NBC. "White Like Me." *Saturday Night Live,* December 15, 1984. https://www.nbc.com/saturday-night-live/video/white-like-me/n9308 [https://perma.cc/VTF7-WBQD].

Nguyen, Viet Thanh. "Asian Americans Are Still Caught in the Trap of the 'Model Minority' Stereotype. And It Creates Inequality for All." *Time,* June 25, 2020. https://time.com/5859206/anti-asian-racism-america/.

Nittle, Nadra Kareem. "What Is a Stereotype?" ThoughtCo., February 4, 2021. https://www.thoughtco.com/what-is-the-meaning-of-stereotype-2834956.

Norris, Michele. "Six Words: 'You've Got To Be Taught' Intolerance." NPR. *Morning Edition,* May 19, 2014. https://www.npr.org/2014/05/19/308296815/six-words-youve-got-to-be-taught-intolerance.

North, Anna. "Claims of 'Sex Addiction' Are a Distraction in the Atlanta Killings." *Vox,* March 18, 2021. https://www.vox.com/22336271/atlanta-shooter-sex-addiction-robert-aaron-long.

OCGA § 17-10-1 (2000).

Page-Gould, Elizabeth et al. "With A Little Help from My Cross-Group Friend: Reducing Anxiety in Intergroup Contexts through Cross-Group Friendships." *Journal of Personality and Social Psychology* 95, (2008): 1080.

Page-Gould, Elizabeth. "The Unhealthy Racist." In *Are We Born Racist? New Insights from Neuroscience and Positive Psychology.* Edited by Jason Marsh et al. Beacon Press, 2010.

Paluck, Elizabeth Levy et al. "Prejudice Reduction: Progress and Challenges." *Annual Review Psychology* 72, (2021): 533.

Park, Ed. "Confronting Anti-Asian Discrimination During the Coronavirus Crisis." *The New Yorker,* March 17, 2020. https://www.newyorker.com/culture/culture-desk/confronting-anti-asian-discrimination-during-the-coronavirus-crisis.

Pauly Morgan, Kathryn et al. "Describing the Emperor's New Clothes: Three Myths of Educational (In-)Equality, The Gender Question in Education." *Theory, Pedagogy and Politics* 105, no. 1 (1996).

Peffer, George Anthony. "Forbidden Families: Emigration Experiences of Chinese Women Under the Page Law, 1875-1882." *Journal of American Ethnic History* 28, (1986): 6.

Peñaloza, Marisa. "'Illicit Cohabitation': Listen To 6 Stunning Moments from Loving v. Virginia." NPR, June 12, 2017. https://www.npr.org/2017/06/12/532123349/illicit-cohabitation-listen-to-6-stunning-moments-from-loving-v-virginia.

Peng, Sheng. "Smashed Windows and Racist Graffiti: Vandals Target Asian Americans Amid Coronavirus." *NBC News,* April 10, 2020. https://www.nbcnews.com/news/asian-america/smashed-windows-racist-graffiti-vandals-target-asian-americans-amid-coronavirus-n1180556.

Petri, Alexandra E. "To Combat Anti-Asian Attacks, New Yorkers Join Neighborhood Watch Patrols." *The New York Times,* April 8, 2021. https://www.nytimes.com/2021/04/08/nyregion/anti-asian-violence-neighborhood-watch.html.

Pettit, Emma. "The Academic Concept Conservative Lawmakers Love to Hate." *Chronicle of Higher Education,* May 12, 2020. https://www.chronicle.com/article/the-academic-concept-conservative-lawmakers-love-to-hate.

Phelps, Edmund S. "The Statistical Theory of Racism and Sexism." *American Economic Review* 62 (1972): 659.

Phillips, Kristine. "'They Look at Me and Think I'm Some Kind of Virus': What It's Like to be Asian During the Coronavirus Pandemic." *USA Today,* March 28, 2020. https://www.usatoday.com/story/news/nation/2020/03/28/coronavirus-racism-asian-americans-report-fear-harassment-violence/2903745001/.

Phillips, Kristine. "'We Just Want to be Safe': Hate Crimes, Harassment of Asian Americans Rise Amid Coronavirus Pandemic." *USA Today,* May 21, 2020. https://www.usatoday.com/story/news/politics/2020/05/20/coronavirus-hate-crimes-against-asian-americans-continue-rise/5212123002/.

Pierce, Charles M. "Black Psychiatry One Year After Miami." *Journal of National Medical Association* 62, (1970): 471-472.

Politi, Daniel. "Donald Trump in Phoenix: Mexicans Are 'Taking Our Jobs' and 'Killing Us.'" *Slate,* July 12, 2015. https://slate.com/news-and-politics/2015/07/donald-trump-in-phoenix-mexicans-are-taking-our-jobs-and-killing-us.html.

Public Broadcasting Service. "A Class Divided." *Frontline.* YouTube, January 18, 2019. https://youtu.be/1mcCLm_LwpE.

Public Broadcasting Service. "Talking to Young Children About Race and Racism." https://www.pbs.org/parents/talking-about-racism.

Raines, Howell. "George Wallace, Segregation Symbol, Dies at 79." *The New York Times,* September 14, 1998. https://www.nytimes.com/1998/09/14/us/george-wallace-segregation-symbol-dies-at-79.html.

Ramirez, Marc and Trevor Hughes, "'Stand Up, Fight Back': Atlanta Rally Decries Anti-Asian Violence, Mourns Spa Shooting Victims." *USA Today,* March 21, 2021. https://www.usatoday.com/story/news/nation/2021/03/20/atlanta-shooting-surveillance-video-aaron-long-march-victims/4780302001/.

Ramirez, Marc. "Asian American Activists Are Demanding Equal Civil Rights, Better Education in Schools After Asian Hate Attacks." *USA Today*, March 26, 2021. https://www.usatoday.com/story/news/nation/2021/03/26/stop-asian-hate-asian-americans-across-us-demand-reforms/6990150002/.

Ramirez, Marc. "Stop Asian Hate, Stop Black Hate, Stop All Hate: Many Americans Call for Unity Against Racism." *USA Today,* March 22, 2021. https://www.usatoday.com/story/news/nation/2021/03/20/atlanta-shootings-see-asian-black-americans-take-white-supremacy/4769268001/.

Ramirez, Marc. "Who Gets to Decide What is Racism, Hate? Atlanta Shootings Renew Debate over White Violence, Privilege." *USA Today,* March 18, 2021. https://www.usatoday.com/story/news/2021/03/18/atlanta-victims-were-killed-white-violence-racism-many-insist/4751240001/.

Ramirez, Steven A. "What We Teach When We Teach About Race: The Problem of Law and Pseudo-Economics." *Journal of Legal Education* 54, (2004): 365.

Rawls, Anne Warfield and Waverly Duck. *Tacit Racism.* University of Chicago Press, 2020.

Restuccia, Andrew. "White House Defends Trump Comments on 'Kung Flu,' Coronavirus Testing." *The Wall Street Journal,* June 22, 2020. https://www.wsj.com/articles/white-house-defends-trump-comments-on-kung-flu-coronavirus-testing-11592867688.

Rivers, Eileen and Thuan Le Elston. "AAPI Pride: Asian and Pacific Islander Heritage Helps Lift America to What It Must Be." *USA Today,* May 17, 2021. https://news.yahoo.com/aapi-pride-asian-pacific-islander-130016737.html.

Robinson, Andrew. "'I Shall Never Forget the Kindness.' How England Helped Albert Einstein Escape Nazi Germany." *Time,* October 1, 2019. https://time.com/5684504/einstein-england/.

Rodgers, Richard and Oscar Hammerstein II. "You've Got to Be Carefully Taught." *South Pacific.* YouTube, August 3, 2018. https://www.youtube.com/watch?v=VPf6ITsjsgk.

Roos, Meghan. "Sheriff's Comments That Atlanta Shooter Had 'Really Bad Day' Sparks Backlash." *Newsweek,* March 17, 2021. https://www.newsweek.com/sheriffs-comments-that-atlanta-shooter-had-really-bad-day-sparks-backlash-1576936.

Rutledge, Njeri. "I Thought I Never Personally Experienced Racism. Then I Realized I Just Normalized It." *USA Today,* September 15, 2020. https://www.usatoday.com/story/opinion/voices/2020/09/15/racism-every-day-black-women-column/5793258002/.

Rutstein, Nathan. *Healing Racism in America: A Prescription for the Disease.* Star Commonwealth, 1993.

S. 2043, 116th Congress, (2019).

S. 937, 117th Congress, (2021); H.R. 6721, 116th Cong. (2020).

S. 937, Covid-19 Hate Crimes Act, 117th Congress (2021-2022).

Saunt, Claudio. "The Invasion of America." *Aeon,* January 7, 2015. https://aeon.co/essays/how-were-1-5-billion-acres-of-land-so-rapidly-stolen.

Savage, Leonard J. "Theory of Statistical Decision." *Journal of the American Statistical Association* 46, (1951): 55.

Savage, Leonard J. *The Foundations of Statistics.* Dover Publications, 1972.

Schaller, Mark and Steven L. Neuberg. "Danger, Disease, and the Nature of Prejudice(s)." *Advances in Experimental Social Psychology* 46, no. 1, (2012): 2.

Schelling, Thomas C. "The Mind as a Consuming Organ." In *The Multiple Self.* Edited by Jon Elster. Cambridge University Press, 1987.

Seligman, Martin E. P. et al. "Positive Education: Positive Psychology and Classroom Interventions" *Oxford Review of Education* 35, (2009): 293.

Selmi, Michael. "The Paradox of Implicit Bias and a Plea for a New Narrative." *Arizona State Law Journal* 50, (2018): 193.

Serwer, Adam. "A Crime by Any Name." *The Atlantic,* July 3, 2019, https://www.theatlantic.com/ideas/archive/2019/07/border-facilities/593239/.

Sharot, Tali and Cass R. Sunstein. "How People Decide What They Want to Know." *Nature Human Behavior* 4, (2020): 14.

Shear, Michael D. "Confronting Violence Against Asians, Biden Says That 'We Cannot Be Complicit.'" *The New York Times*, March 19, 2021. https://www.nytimes.com/2021/03/19/us/politics/biden-harris-atlanta.html.

Shiller, Robert J. "Narrative Economics." *American Economic Review* 107, (2017): 967.

Shiller, Robert J. *Narrative Economics: How Stories Go Viral and Drive Major Economic Events.* Princeton University Press, 2019.

Shin, Heidi. "I'm Helping My Korean-American Daughter Embrace Her Identity to Counter Racism." *The New York Times,* March 19, 2021. https://www.nytimes.com/2021/03/19/well/family/Talking-to-children-anti-Asian-bias.html.

Silverthorn, Michelle. "5 Ways Law Students Can Interrupt Implicit Bias, Diversity." Student Lawyer Blog. American Bar Association. May 29, 2018. https://abaforlawstudents.com/2018/05/29/5-ways-law-students-can-interrupt-implicit-bias/.

Simpkins, Kelsey. "Anti-Asian Discrimination Amid Pandemic Spurs Jennifer Ho to Action." *CU Boulder Today,* April 17, 2020. https://www.colorado.edu/today/2020/04/17/anti-asian-discrimination-amid-pandemic-spurs-jennifer-ho-action.

Simpson, Kelly. "Chinese Americans: Remembering a Golden Legacy." KCET. January 24, 2012. https://www.kcet.org/history-society/chinese-americans-remembering-a-golden-legacy.

Sisak, Michael R. and Karen Matthews. "Video Shows Vicious Attack of Asian American Woman in NYC." *Associated Press News,* March 30, 2021. https://apnews.com/article/65-year-old-asian-woman-assaulted-nyc-street-692b82db37efae29d12e7fa638eb2e1d.

Slave Voyages, website. https://www.slavevoyages.org/.

Spence, Michael. "Job Market Signaling." *Quarterly Journal of Economics* 87, (1973): 355, 368–374.

Spriggs, William. "A Teachable Moment? Will George Floyd's Death Spur Change in Economics?" Federal Reserve Bank of Minneapolis, June 9, 2020. https://www.minneapolisfed.org/article/2020/a-teachable-moment-will-george-floyds-death-spur-change-in-economics.

Staff Writer. "What Is a Microaggression?" *Psychology Today.* https://www.psychologytoday.com/us/basics/microaggression.

Stanchi, Kathryn. "The Rhetoric of Racism in the United States Supreme Court." *Boston College Law Review* 62, (2021): 1251.

State v. Bridges 133 N.J. 447 (1993) 628 A.2d 270.

Staughton, John. "Why Do People Have Different Skin Colors?" *Science ABC,* January 18, 2021. https://www.scienceabc.com/humans/melanin-pigment-definition-meaning-skin-color.html.

Stiglitz, Joseph E. "Approaches to the Economics of Discrimination." *American Economic Review* 63, (1973): 287.

Sue, Derald Wing and Lisa Spanierman. *Microaggressions in Everyday Life: Race, Gender, and Sexual Orientation.* Wiley, 2010.

Sue, Derald Wing et al. "Racial Microaggressions in Everyday Life: Implications for Clinical Practice." *American Psychologist* 62, (2007): 271.

Summer, Leonard Wayne. "Hate Crimes, Literature, and Speech." In *A Companion to Applied Ethics.* Edited by R. G. Frey and Christopher Heath Wellman. Wiley-Blackwell, 2005.

Sun, Rebecca. "Comedian Jenny Yang Rebuts Andrew Yang Op-Ed with Satirical Video: 'Honk If You Won't Hate-Crime Me!'" *Hollywood Reporter,* April 5, 2020. https://www.hollywoodreporter.com/news/comedian-jenny-yang-rebuts-andrew-yang-op-ed-satirical-video-1288623.

Swisher, Kara. "An Asian American Poet on Refusing to Take Up 'Apologetic Space.'" *The New York Times,* April 1, 2021. https://www.nytimes.com/2021/04/01/opinion/sway-kara-swisher-cathy-park-hong.html.

Szalai, Jennifer. "'The Sum of Us' Tallies the Cost of Racism for Everyone." *The New York Times*, February 23, 2021. https://www.nytimes.com/2021/02/23/books/review-sum-of-us-heather-mcghee.html.

Tahmasbi, Fatemeh et al. "'Go Eat a Bat, Chang!': On the Emergence of Sinophobic Behavior on Web Communities in the Face of Covid-19." Cornell University, *ArXiv,* March 3, 2021. https://arxiv.org/abs/2004.04046.

Takei, George. Twitter, April 7, 2020. https://twitter.com/GeorgeTakei/status/1246139544115777542.

Tang, Crystal. "Unpacking the Model Minority Myth." Beneficial State Foundation, June 4, 2019. https://beneficialstate.org/perspectives/unpacking-the-model-minority-myth/.

Tavernise, Sabrina and Richard A. Oppel Jr. "Spit On, Yelled At, Attacked: Chinese-Americans Fear for Their Safety." *The New York Times,* March 23, 2021. https://www.nytimes.com/2020/03/23/us/chinese-coronavirus-racist-attacks.html.

The Late Show with Stephen Colbert. "Keegan-Michael Key: My Encounters with Police Are Different As a Famous Black Man." YouTube, June 3, 2020. https://youtu.be/2A6I_a3EJwc.

Timberg, Craig and Allyson Chiu. "As the Coronavirus Spreads, So Does Online Racism Targeting Asians, New Research Shows." *The Washington Post,* April 8, 2020. https://www.washingtonpost.com/technology/2020/04/08/coronavirus-spreads-so-does-online-racism-targeting-asians-new-research-shows/.

Torres, Stacy. "Violence and Hate Against Asian Americans is a Health and Safety Crisis for Everyone." *USA Today,* March 18, 2021. https://www.freep.com/story/opinion/2021/03/17/anti-asian-violence-covid-safety-crisis-hurts-everyone-column/4736733001/.

Treisman, Rachel. "Attack on Asian Woman in Manhattan, as Bystanders Watched, To Be Probed as Hate Crime." NPR, March 30, 2021, https://www.npr.org/2021/03/30/982745950/attack-on-asian-woman-in-manhattan-as-bystanders-watched-to-be-probed-as-hate-cr.

Tully, Tracey. "Debate Erupts at N.J. Law School After White Student Quotes Racial Slur." *The New York Times*, May 3, 2021. https://www.nytimes.com/2021/05/03/nyregion/Rutgers-law-school-n-word.html.

Twain, Mark. *Following the Equator: A Journey Around the World.* Public Domain, 1897. https://www.gutenberg.org/files/2895/2895-h/2895-h.htm.

US Bureau of Labor Statistics. "Asian Women and Men Earned More Than Their White, Black, and Hispanic Counterparts in 2017." August 29, 2018. https://www.bls.gov/opub/ted/2018/asian-women-and-men-earned-more-than-their-white-black-and-hispanic-counterparts-in-2017.htm.

United States Courts. "History—Brown v. Board of Education Re-Enactment." https://www.uscourts.gov/educational-resources/educational-activities/history-brown-v-board-education-re-enactment.

United States Department of Justice. Bureau of Justice Assistance. "A Policymakers' Guide to Hate Crimes." March 1997.

United States Department of Justice. Civil Rights Division, "Hate Crime Laws." https://www.justice.gov/crt/hate-crime-laws.

United States Department of Justice. Civil Rights Division. "Laws and Policies." https://www.justice.gov/hatecrimes/laws-and-policies.

United States Department of Justice. Civil Rights Division. "Learn More About Hate Crimes." https://www.justice.gov/hatecrimes/learn-about-hate-crimes/chart.

University of Connecticut School of Law. "Implicit Bias in the Courts." https://libguides.law.uconn.edu/implicit/courts.18 U.S.C. § 249 (2009).

Varian, Hal. "Equity, Envy, and Efficiency." *Journal of Economic Theory* 9, (1974): 63.

Victor, Daniel. "Georgia Added a Hate-Crimes Law Last Year After the Death of Ahmaud Arbery." *The New York Times*, March 18, 2021. https://www.nytimes.com/2021/03/18/us/georgia-hate-crime-law.html.

Vigdor, Neil. "Attack on Asian Woman in Midtown Prompts Another Hate Crime Investigation." *The New York Times,* March 31, 2021. https://www.nytimes.com/2021/03/30/nyregion/attack-asian-woman-midtown.html.

Volokh, Eugene. "Rutgers Law Students Calling for a 'Policy' on Students and Faculty Quoting Slurs from Court Cases." Volokh Conspiracy. May 3, 2021. https://reason.com/volokh/2021/05/03/rutgers-law-students-calling-for-a-policy-on-students-and-faculty-quoting-slurs-from-court-cases/.

Wallace, Kelly. "Forgotten Los Angeles History: The Chinese Massacre of 1871." Los Angeles Public Library, May 19, 2017. https://www.lapl.org/collections-resources/blogs/lapl/chinese-massacre-1871.

Wang, Jenny T. *Permission to Come Home: Reclaiming Mental Health as Asian Americans.* Balance, 2022.

Warfare History Network. "Hitler's Biggest Mistake: Why the Nazi Atomic Bomb Never Happened." National Interest. October 16, 2020. https://nationalinterest.org/blog/buzz/hitlers-biggest-mistake-why-nazi-atomic-bomb-never-happened-170800/.

Wei, William. "The Chinese-American Experience: An Introduction." *Harper's Weekly.* https://immigrants.harpweek.com/ChineseAmericans/1Introduction/BillWeiIntro.htm.

Weise, Elizabeth. "Anti-Asian Hashtags Soared After Donald Trump First Tied Covid-19 to China on Twitter, Study Shows." *USA Today,* March 18, 2021. https://www.usatoday.com/story/news/nation/2021/03/18/anti-asian-hashtags-donald-trump-covid-19-tweet-study/4728444001/.

Weiss, Debra Cassens. "11% of Law Students Had Suicidal Thoughts in the Past Year, Survey Finds; What Can Law Schools Do?" *American Bar Association Journal,* (July 14, 2022). https://www.abajournal.com/web/article/11-of-law-students-had-suicidal-thoughts-in-the-past-year-survey-finds-what-can-law-schools-do.

Weiss, Debra Cassens. "Law Student Who Quoted from Opinion, Including its Racial Slur, Finds Herself at Center of Controversy." *American Bar Association Journal,* May 4, 2021. https://www.abajournal.com/news/article/law-student-who-quoted-from-opinion-including-its-racial-slur-finds-herself-at-center-of-controversy.

Wheaton, Elizabeth M. *The Economics of Human Rights.* Routledge, 2018.

White House. "A Proclamation on Asian American and Native Hawaiian / Pacific Islander Heritage Month, 2021." April 30, 2021. https://www.whitehouse.gov/briefing-room/presidential-actions/2021/04/30/a-proclamation-on-asian-american-and-native-hawaiian-pacific-islander-heritage-month-2021/.

Wilson, Timothy D. and Daniel T. Gilbert. "Explaining Away: A Model of Affective Adaptation." *Perspectives on Psychological Science* 3, (2008): 370.

Wisconsin v. Mitchell, 508 U.S. 476, 479 (1993).

Wong, Alia. "Teaching Kids to Hate America? Republicans Want 'Critical Race Theory' Out of Schools." *USA Today*, May 13, 2021. https://www.usatoday.com/story/news/education/2021/05/13/republicans-seek-stop-schools-teaching-critical-race-theory/4993370001//.

Wong, Alia. "Why Schools Are Banning Yoga." *The Atlantic,* September 20, 2018. https://www.theatlantic.com/education/archive/2018/09/why-schools-are-banning-yoga/570904/.

Wong, Charlene. "Fancy Terminology." Judge-Me-Not: By My Circumstances (website). https://judge-me-not.weebly.com/fancy-terminology.html.

World Health Organization, "WHO Issues Best Practices for Naming New Human Infectious Diseases." May 8, 2015. https://www.who.int/news/item/08-05-2015-who-issues-best-practices-for-naming-new-human-infectious-diseases.

Wright, Robert. *The Moral Animal: Why We Are the Way We Are: The New Science of Evolutionary Psychology.* Vintage Press, 1995.

Wu, Constance. *Making a Scene.* New York: Scribner, 2022.

Wu, Constance. Twitter, July 14, 2022. https://twitter.com/ConstanceWu/status/1547661204545359877/.

Wu, Ellen D. "Asian Americans and the 'Model Minority' Myth." *Los Angeles Times,* January 23, 2014. https://www.latimes.com/opinion/op-ed/la-oe-0123-wu-chua-model-minority-chinese-20140123-story.html.

Wu, Ellen D. *The Color of Success: Asian Americans and the Origins of the Model Minority.* Princeton University Press, 2015.

Wu, Frank H. "Asian Americans and the Future of Civil Rights." Society of American Law Teachers, webinar, May 25, 2021. https://www.saltlaw.org/video-now-available-asian-americans-and-the-future-of-civil-rights/.

Wu, Frank H. "Why Vincent Chin Matters." *The New York Times,* June 22, 2012. https://www.nytimes.com/2012/06/23/opinion/why-vincent-chin-matters.html.

Wu, Kathy. "Assume Every Child Has PTSD These Days Until Proven Otherwise." MedPage Today, May 28, 2022.

Yam, Kimmy. "There Were 3,800 Anti-Asian Racist Incidents, Mostly Against Women, in Past Year." *NBC News,* March 16, 2021. https://www.nbcnews.com/news/asian-america/there-were-3-800-anti-asian-racist-incidents-mostly-against-n1261257.

Yang, Andrew. "Andrew Yang: We Asian Americans Are Not the Virus, but We Can Be Part of the Cure." *The Washington Post,* April 1, 2020. https://www.washingtonpost.com/opinions/2020/04/01/andrew-yang-coronavirus-discrimination/.

Yang, Jeff. "A New Virus Stirs Up Ancient Hatred." CNN, January 30, 2020. https://www.cnn.com/2020/01/30/opinions/wuhan-coronavirus-is-fueling-racism-xenophobia-yang/index.html.

Yang, Jenny. Twitter. April 3, 2020. https://twitter.com/jennyyangtv/status/1246132396191178752.

Yeomans, Michael, Maurice E. Schweitzer, and Alison Wood Brooks. "The Conversational Circumplex: Identifying, Prioritizing, and Pursuing Informational and Relational Motives in Conversation." *Current Opinions in Psychology* 44, (2022): 302.

Yeun, Steven. Twitter, April 3, 2020. https://twitter.com/steveyeun/status/1246186737455357952.

Yoo, Paula. *From a Whisper to A Rallying Cry: The Killing of Vincent Chin and the Trial That Galvanized the Asian American Movement.* Norton Young Readers, 2021.

Yoshiko Kandil, Caitlin. "Asian Americans Report Over 650 Racist Acts Over Last Week, New Data Says." *NBC News,* March 26, 2020. https://www.nbcnews.com/news/asian-america/asian-americans-report-nearly-500-racist-acts-over-last-week-n1169821.

Young, Damon. "The Definition, Danger and Disease of Respectability Politics, Explained." *The Root,* March 21, 2016. https://www.theroot.com/the-definition-danger-and-disease-of-respectdability-po-1790854699.

Zeki, Semir and John Paul Romaya. "Neural Correlates of Hate." *PLOS One* 3, (2008): e3556.

Zhang, Melody. "Don't Overlook the Virulence of Racism Toward Asian Americans." *Sojourners*, March 26, 2020. https://sojo.net/articles/don-t-overlook-virulence-racism-toward-asian-americans.

Ziv, Avner. "Teaching and Learning with Humor: Experiment and Replication." *Journal of Experimental Education* 57, (1988): 5.

Index